THE BEST OF
BENTINE

By the same author

THE LONG BANANA SKIN
MADAME'S GIRLS
THE DOOR MARKED SUMMER
SMITH & SON REMOVERS

THE BEST OF BENTINE

Michael Bentine

Illustrated by the author

GRANADA
London Toronto Sydney New York

Granada Publishing Limited
Frogmore, St Albans, Herts AL2 2NF
and
36 Golden Square, London W1R 4AH
515 Madison Avenue, New York, NY 10022, USA
117 York Street, Sydney, NSW 2000, Australia
60 International Blvd, Rexdale, Ontario, R9W 6J2, Canada
61 Beach Road, Auckland, New Zealand

Published by Granada Publishing 1983

British Library Cataloguing in Publication Data

Bentine, Michael
  The best of Bentine
  I. Title
  828'.91407   PR6052.E/

ISBN 0 246 11843 1

Typeset by A-Line Services, Saffron Walden, Essex
Printed and bound in Great Britain by
Mackays of Chatham Ltd

Granada ®
Granada Publishing ®

CONTENTS

To my good friend Peter Sellers
who gave the joy of laughter to millions
by his great comedy talent

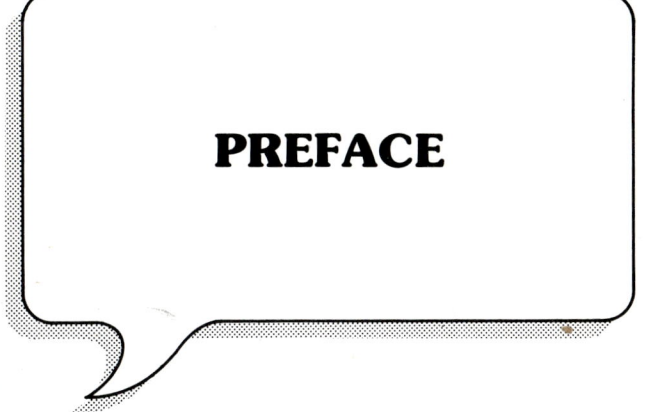

PREFACE

You can tell a hundred people a sad story and get approximately the same reaction from all of them, but tell a 'funny' story to a hundred people and you get a hundred totally different reactions. These range from a hysterical appreciation of the joke to a blank stare of incomprehension.

Put those same hundred people together in an audience and once again the reactions change, but the results can be explosive. Screams of laughter or a deafening silence. Generally, the tighter-packed the auditorium the greater the audience reaction becomes; a thin house is definitely harder to work to than a full one. Yet even if you can command only fifty per cent of your audience, you will get the roars of laughter that make it all worthwhile, especially if you have written your act yourself, as I always have.

Cabaret is different. The audience is split into small clumps, seated round tables, usually eating indifferent food and paying exorbitant prices for inferior drinks. In those conditions, cabaret is bloody hard work. In the 'good old days' of variety and vaudeville a fifteen-minute act was considered a long one. In cabaret you have to do an hour. Years ago, the comedian had to 'get' the audience in the first few minutes of his act or he 'died' standing up.

I've 'died' many times in many places – but in others, by some strange chemistry, I've 'wowed 'em', had them 'rolling in the aisles', and left 'not a dry seat in the house'. All these idiotic clichés do sum up the feeling of elated relief as your hyper-adrenalated self takes the calls at the end of an act that leaves you drenched in dishonest sweat. The saying 'Comedy is ten per cent inspiration and ninety per cent perspiration' is an accurate summation – no matter how hackneyed.

Whether or not you find this book funny is entirely up to you, but I do make one claim for this material. All these pieces have been successful on radio, stage or cabaret, and some of them have worked on the big screen. I hope that reading them (aloud, please, if possible) will give as much pleasure to you as I have had in devising them.

I had just come back from the Second World War. My parents welcomed me into their small apartment near Hammersmith Bridge and helped me to overcome some of the ravages of war, but sleep was made even more difficult by the intrusion of an insect which had made its home somewhere in the cavity walls of their apartment.

THE TCK-TCK EXTERMINATOR

It was a cricket and 'Tcked-Tcked' its maddening communications all through the night. By the end of twenty-four hours my already ragged nerves were in shreds. Pop rang up the local borough offices and explained the situation. Within an hour a pest exterminator had arrived. He brought with him a large official truck and two assistants plus a mass of heavy equipment, which collectively I guessed would have tipped the scales at about half a ton. They were obviously well equipped to deal with any kind of infestation from rattlesnakes to death-watch beetles. The apartment was on the second floor, so a preliminary reconnaissance was called for before the appropriate equipment could be lugged up the stairs.

The disinfestation procedure would nowadays be described as 'overkill'. It consisted mainly of a pump filled with powder and equipped with a long flexible nozzle and various large kinds of insect repellent plus two cylinders of some sort of noxious gas.

The head exterminator was an enormous grey-haired yeoman of advanced middle-age with hands like a gorilla. He gave an impression of tremendous physical power and dedicated professional determination.

His two assistants, who were totally dominated by their chief's sheer physical presence, left little impression on me other than that they seemed to hang on to their master's every word. They were merely the tool passers, the instrument carriers, and nothing more.

The grizzled exterminator – victor of thousands of efficient exterminations – was himself equipped with an ancient stethoscope, which he hung round his neck like a medical consultant.

'Where is the little creature?' he asked in a let's-waste-no-time tone of voice.

'I don't know. The little bastard seems to be everywhere.'

'Typical,' he replied with the confidence of a specialist. 'The common cricket seems a deceptively easy insect to locate until you actually try to pinpoint it. Not an easy job you know – takes years of experience. You have to get to know your enemy – get inside the cricket's mind, as it were.'

1

'Quite,' I said tersely.

'We'll have him pinned down in no time,' added the bulky exterminator. He was over-optimistic. It took nearly three hours before he finally made a chalk circle on the wall of the kitchen to indicate the target area. 'Got him,' he said loudly.

An assistant handed him a brace and bit and the chief carefully drilled into the plaster. He then inserted the long tube of the large powder pump, which closely resembled the stirrup arrangement of the civil defence fire appliances.

'This will do the trick,' he said, smiling for the first time, and the extermination commenced.

The results were dramatic in the extreme. After five minutes energetic pumping by the second assistant a loud hollow groan issued from the apartment below. This was followed by a ghastly choking sound and the dull thump of a body falling unconscious to the floor.

'My God,' I said hoarsely. 'It's the little old lady underneath – she's a chronic asthmatic.'

We got to her just in time by forcing her front door. Her apartment was filled with dusty fog and the poor old dear was alone and near to passing away. We opened all the windows and fanned away the cloud of airborne insect powder which had leaked from a crack in the plaster above the fireplace. By this time Mother and Pop had returned from shopping and they both stayed with the comatose old lady till the doctor arrived.

Meanwhile, upstairs in our apartment the battle seemed to be over. I congratulated the extermination team and gave them a drink.

'It's never easy,' said the chief with a modest air of achievement. 'You've got to know their habits. Little sods they are.'

As if in agreement and clear as a bell the cricket cricked 'Tck-Tck' twice.

In all it took three days and a second extermination team before the noisy intruder finally succumbed. God knows what it cost, apart from the near loss of my reason and the risk of one little old lady's life.

Fifteen years later I wrote this sketch.

A confident Master of Ceremonies acknowledges the applause of the studio audience as he steps up to the microphone.

MC: *(Smiling broadly to display his expensive expanse of porcelain crowns)* Hello there! And a warm welcome to our show. *(At this point he is interrupted by the loud chirrup of a cricket)*

CRICKET: Tck-Tck.

MC: *(Hurriedly covering up for the apparent 'glitch' in the sound system)* Once again we proudly present a line-up of stars . . . *(And once again the cricket interrupts)*

CRICKET: Tck-Tck.

MC: *(His smile becomes a little less confident but he is still very much in command)* I'm sorry about that. It appears that we have a little problem here. We seem to have a . . .

CRICKET: *(On cue)* Tck-Tck.

MC: . . . in the studio. *(He now incorporates the cricket sound into his pattern of speech)*

CRICKET: Tck-Tck.

MC: Yes, indeed we do. At this time of the year, not infrequently, one finds . . .

CRICKET: Tck-Tck.

MC: *(Continuing unabashed)* . . . s in the studio equipment. Especially in these older studios. *(He shouts off microphone)* Hey, Mack! Can we do something about this? We've got a . . .

CRICKET: Tck-Tck.

MC: . . . in the system.

VOICE OFF: OK. We've sent for the exterminator. He'll be right there.

MC: I really must apologize for the delay in presenting our show, but as you just heard a . . .

CRICKET: Tck-Tck.

MC: . . . exterminator is on the way. And shortly . . .

(The MC is interrupted by the arrival of the Tck-Tck Exterminator, who is dressed in blue overalls and a bowler hat and is carrying a heavy back-pack containing a massive battery and various drills, etc. Clamped over his bowler hat is a pair of earphones and on top of the crown of the 'Derby' is a small radar aerial)

EXTERMINATOR: *(Presenting his card)* Have no worry. Have no fear. Your friendly neighbourhood . . .

CRICKET: Tck-Tck.

EXTERMINATOR: . . . exterminating man is here. My card.

MC: *(Taking card)* Thank you. *(Reads it)* Fred Bogg.

CRICKET: Tck-Tck.

MC: Exterminations a speciality. Well! That's just fine. Please get on with it. We have a show to do.

EXTERMINATOR (FRED): Right! Now, where is the little . . .

CRICKET: Tck-Tck.

EXTERMINATOR (FRED): . . . located?

MC: *(Getting exasperated at the delay)* I don't know. The sound seems to be everywhere.

FRED: I thought so. We've got a really tough customer to deal with. What we in the profession call a maverick . . .

CRICKET: Tck-Tck.

FRED: He knows we know, you know.

MC: *(Losing his cool)* Just get rid of the little . . .

CRICKET: Tck-Tck.

MC: . . . that's all.

FRED: Right. I'll use my high frequency . . .

CRICKET: Tck-Tck.

FRED: . . . detector.

(From his back-pack Fred the Exterminator pulls out a short metal detector with a telescopic handle, and adjusts it)

FRED: For this part of the operation I shall require absolute silence please.

(A cough sounds)

FRED: Please! Absolute hush if you please.

(Another cough or sneeze is heard)

FRED: Please! I cannot conduct the extermination procedure without complete quiet. In other words – in professional parlance – keep dead *stumm*. Thank you.

(Fred now moves around the set, swinging his detector from side to side, until he comes to a table. At this point the cricket cricks with almost obscene clarity.)

FRED: That's him. Quick! Hand me my drill, while I hold him in conversation. *(He turns to where the cricket is located)* I know you're in there you little . . .
CRICKET: Tck-Tck.
FRED: You!

(By this time the MC has found the electric drill in Fred's back-pack and has handed it to him. Fred immediately drills a hole in the table top and blows the sawdust away – leaning right over the hole and looking down it, like a man at a vertical keyhole)

FRED: Hello my little . . .
CRICKET: Tck-Tck.
FRED: You're a pretty little . . .
CRICKET: Tck-Tck.
FRED: Aren't you? I can see you. Yes I can. *(Fred has adopted the sort of voice people use when chatting up extremely young babies)* Who's a lovely hairy little . . .
CRICKET: Tck-Tck.
FRED: There, eh? *(He covers the drill hole with his hand and in a stage whisper addresses the MC)* Quick! Get my gun while I divert his attention. *(He turns back and bends down again speaking gently through the drill hole)* Uncle's got something for you, my little . . .
CRICKET: Tck-Tck.
FRED: Yes, he has. *(By this time he is holding a .38 revolver, handed to him by the MC)* Hold very still my pretty little . . .
CRICKET: Tck-Tck.
FRED: There's a good boy. *(Fred looks closer)* Sorry, girl.

(Fred fires two shots straight down the drill hole)

CRICKET: Tck-Tck. Tck-Tck.

(The agonized sound of a dying cricket is heard in all its heart-rending pathetic majesty)

FRED: *(As sound of dying cricket finally ceases – the cricket being a bit of a ham, this can take some time)* She's gone!

(He turns to the audience, his face working with emotion)

FRED: *(With feeling)* I hate my work.

(He bursts into tears and staggers off, a broken man)

MC: *(Disgustedly)* It's just not cricket.

I got into serious trouble in 1963 at the Montreux Television Festival. It was all quite innocent, really. The BBC had given me the opportunity to have a go at the Montreux Light Entertainment Prize, the Golden Rose of Television.

In 1960, the BBC had won the competition for the Best Light Entertainment Programme with *The Black and White Minstrel Show*, which was a simple two-camera recording of a played-back song and dance show. My own show was called *It's a Square World* and it won the Grand Prix de la Presse. It might have won the Golden Rose, but I made the unwitting mistake of showing a trick film of the United Nations singing and dancing to the Russian tune 'Black Eyes', while Khrushchev apparently beat time with his shoe. The film was all brilliantly cut together by my editor Jim Latham (who edited Carl Sagan's *Cosmos*), and was as gentle a send-up as one could wish. It was clean, too.

The judge who disliked it was at Montreux for the first time, and he was a Russian! I quite see that he could hardly support that sort of thing, so he put the veto on the judges' verdict.

Emboldened by that essay into gentle satire, I wrote this sketch for the following season.

UNO CARPETS

A section of one of those multiple rostrums on which the delegates are placed, seated behind long desks. Their national emblems are displayed in miniature alongside a discreet notice identifying their country of origin. The British delegate is next to the French delegate, then comes the East German and, on the end of that particular rostrum, the United Arab Republic's delegate. The Security Council is in full session and the Arab delegate is standing up making an impassioned reply to some motion on the floor.

The British, French and German delegates are all idly listening to their interpreters through headphones and making notes on their pads.

ARAB: Al ill achmar bala mala kolaba eesh mal man habla nalla da mill-mill muklan . . . *(He babbles on volubly in 'Arabic')*

(A phone rings on the UK portion of the desk and the British delegate picks it up and quietly answers it. He is obviously somewhat put out by the interruption)

BRITISH DELEGATE: Humphrey Blackstone here. What? Oh darling! *(Fiercely)* I told you not to ring me here during working hours. *(The conversation is conducted in intense whispers)* You've done what? Bought a new drawing-room carpet? *(He speaks loudly so that for a moment the French delegate's attention is drawn to him)* How much? For a bloody carpet! That's ridiculous! I don't care if it *is* the finest Axminster. Two thousand quid is daylight robbery!

(The French delegate can't help listening to this conversation, which must be more interesting than the endless platitudes coming from the United Arab Republic delegate. The British delegate has an inspiration)

BLACKSTONE: Hang on a minute, darling. *(He puts his hand over the telephone and turns to his French colleague)* I say, Dulac, old boy. How much would you have to pay for a French drawing-room carpet?
DULAC: How big?
BLACKSTONE: *(Turning to phone)* How big, darling? The carpet – how big is it? *(Turns back to Dulac)* About eighteen feet by twelve feet. *(Counts on his fingers)* That's about six metres by four metres.
DULAC: *(Scribbling it down)* C'est à dire six mètres par quatre mètres. Un moment, Humphrey. *(He picks up his phone)* 'Allo! *(All this continues in sotto voce)* I'm calling my home in Paris. Oh! 'Allo! Donnez-moi immédiatement Paris, numéro dix-sept soixante et un, quarante-trois double zéro!

(We hear the phone ring and an immediate click as the receiver is lifted in Paris)

DULAC: *(Warmly)* 'Allo, Brigitte! Chérie! Comment vas-tu, mon petit chou? Oui, naturellement, c'est moi, Alphonse, ton petit Alphonse. Oui, Coco. Je t'adore. *(Turns back to Blackstone)* It's the maid. 'Allo, oui! Si je peux parler avec ma femme. Bon, moi aussi. *(His tone changes to one of subdued husbandly affection)* 'Allo, chérie. Oui, c'est moi. Bon. Tout va bien? Et les enfants, hein? Bon. Chérie, c'est plus important. Combien ça coute, par exemple, un tapis de bonne qualité, à peu près de six mètres par quatre mètres? Eh? Pour le salon d'un ami à moi. Environ quinze mille francs? Merci beaucoup, chérie. Oui, je t'aime. Au revoir! *(He puts down the phone and in a rather louder natural tone says to Blackstone)* Cécile, my wife, says she can get you a carpet for around fifteen thousand francs – that's *(He makes a quick calculation)* about fifteen hundred pounds sterling.

(All this time the Arab delegate has been droning on unmusically and graphically making his points, and the German delegate has now been following the Dulac phone conversation and his French colleague's last remarks. Suddenly he interrupts)

GERMAN DELEGATE: Dat's a pretty fancy price for an ordinary French carpet, Dulac! I'm sure we could do better, Blackstone, *(He leans over Dulac)* in Berlin.

DULAC: I'm speaking about a first-class quality copy of a Gobelin carpet, Rumplemeier. Not some synthetic German ersatz man-made-fibre floor-mat. It's all wool, Rumplemeier, pure French virgin wool.

RUMPLEMEIER: *(To Blackstone)* Moths! Dat's vot you get mit wool – moths! I tell you, Herr Blackstone, Dulac is trying to sell you a typically French overpriced article. I personally, Otto von Rumplemeier, guarantee *(His voice has now risen and he is ranting in his enthusiasm)* to get you a carpet – first class, number von quality, like de Führer himself used to eat – for *(Thinks)* four thousand Deutsche Marks. Dat's under one thousand pounds sterling. Beat dat, froggie!
(He snarls his last remark at Dulac)

(The Arab delegate stops in mid-harangue, listening to the German's tirade. Then, he whips out three small carpets from underneath his burnous)

ARAB: I can give you best-quality carpet for half de price. Only five hundred pounds! I take Master Card, Visa, Diners, even cash.

(We cut to various stock shots of the famous faces at the United Nations with appropriate dialogue)
  'I'll take one.'
  'Do you take luncheon vouchers?'
  'How about a reduction for quantity?'
  'OK, Abdul, mark me down for three.' etc.
And fade out on the general scene of excited bartering with the Arab delegate producing carpets from behind his desk and acknowledging the bidding)

ARAB: One for you, Mr President. Two for you, Mr Prime Minister. Four for you, Your Excellency. Certainly, Your Highness. American Express? Dat will do nicely.

Traditional national games are always a delight, especially Olde Englishe ones. They have about them the dedicated air of an ancient amateurism that sets them apart from the crass commercialism of today's sport. Royal tennis, with its cries of 'Royal Chase', is played on a court which is an outline replica of the stables in the Tuileries in Paris. To the uninitiated it is quite incomprehensible.

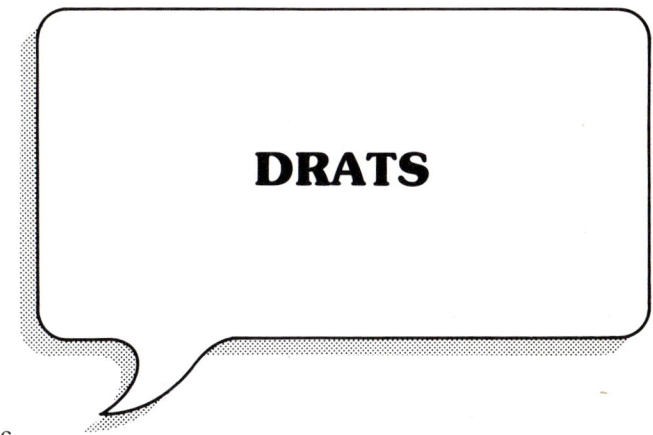

British pub-games are in this category of pastimes whose origins go far back into the past and generally started as something else. Darts is an example. Originally British inns (in those days English inns) were the site for the enforced regulation archery practice that each yeoman archer had to complete every weekend. When the bow ceased to be the prime weapon of imperialist aggression, and the archer was superseded by the musketeer, the weekly 'shoot' became miniaturized and moved inside the inn. So the game of darts was born.

One day I was explaining the vagaries of British pub sports to Dick Lester, my director for many television shows in the late fifties. Being American, Dick was fascinated by pastimes, and when I told him about a misprint in a local paper referring to a darts match as a 'drats' match, he asked me if I was quite sure that 'drats' wasn't actually an ancient British game.

Then and there I adlibbed what a 'drats' match would be like, and that weekend I wrote the sketch in the form which has since been used on television, stage and radio. It caught the public fancy and large numbers of local pubs started to play 'drats', using God alone knows what home-made rules.

The real reason for this 'revival' of a non-existent sport was the excuse it gave to extend drinking hours. However, the performance of these ancient rites gave a great deal of innocent pleasure to the devotees of public-house activities.

Long may it continue to do so.

A typical Olde Englishe pub. Low beams and a smoke-darkened plaster ceiling are hung with horse-brasses and decorated with old pewter tankards and rusty horse-shoes. The pub is filled with yeomen in their traditional garb of flannel shirts and knotted red-spotted handkerchiefs, while their moleskin trousers are held up above their yeoman boots with knotted string. One or two of the local yeomen are holding ten-foot poles, gaily painted with stripes. Behind the bar is a purple-nosed, bloated landlord and a cheerful, buxom barmaid, giggling away and slapping the odd rustic whose questing hands stray over the contours of her fulsome figure.

The chatter is incoherently 'Mummerset', with the lilting burr of the south-western counties of 'Olde Englande'. It is loudly animated and only interrupted by the heavy slurps of 'rough' cider that is being consumed by the gallon. The bar is decorated with bunting, and a large sign which reads 'Annual Drats Match' hangs prominently in one corner. Into the bar comes a stranger and the buzz of cheerful banter ceases as though cut off with a knife. The newcomer is obviously a 'Townee'.

STRANGER: Good evening! *(He walks up to the bar and addresses the waistcoated bulky figure in shirt-sleeves behind the beer pumps)* Are you the landlord?

LANDLORD: Ah! And what if I am?

STRANGER: I'm Charles Berkeley, from the BBC. *(He looks round haught-ily)*

(A reverent murmur of appropriate awe comes from the customers)

LANDLORD: *(Thawing slightly)* Oh! *Be* you now! And what brings 'ee to these 'ere parts of ourn?

BERKELEY: I'm surveying the local country pubs for a programme we're doing on pub-games and sports, and I see by the local paper that your pub, the Ruptured Pig, specializes in the game of drats.

LANDLORD: *(Amid proud cries and murmurs of assent)* Ah, drats! The Game of Games! Greatest pub-game in Olde Englande!

(Cries of Ah! Ooh! Ee! 'Er be that! Drats – 'mazin' game, noble, aah 'tis, etc.)

BERKELEY: Have you been playing drats for long?

(This convulses the landlord who chortles happily amid general guffaws of cidery laughter)

LANDLORD: Aah! Oh! Ho! Ho! Ho! Oh! Ah! *(He goes on laughing heartily till his eyes water and he is forced to wipe them on his spotted handkerchief. He makes up for the liquid tears with a hearty swig of cider)* Ho! Ho! Ho! *(Pause)* . . . or even longer!

(General cries of hearty rural laughter and rustic mirth ending with massed swigs of cider and the concerted response:)

ALL IN BAR: Or even longer! Ah!

(The BBC man is a bit confused but presses on regardless)

BERKELEY: I wonder if you could explain the game of drats to me? So I can get some idea of how it's played. I'll record you.

(The landlord has now come out from behind the bar and stands revealed in high-braced and massively-belted corduroys and heavy boots, just like his customers'. Obviously he enjoys great respect from his patrons as an authority on drats)

LANDLORD: Oh! Ah, drats! 'Er be a noble sport! Sport of kings, dukes, earls and the loike, 'er be.

VARIOUS VOICES: Ah, you tell 'em, Tom! Drats! Cor bless my bedsocks! You tell 'em, Tom!

LANDLORD: Now drats! That is to say, the Great Game . . .*(His eyes are raised reverently and the yeomen take off their hats)* has been goin' on 'ere at the Ruptured Pig for yearn! And yearn! And yearn! And yearn! And yearn! And yearn!

(Suddenly they all stop 'yearning' and together take a long pull at their cider, emptying their glasses)

ALL: Ah! Yearn!

LANDLORD: *(Pointedly)* They're dry! *(Pronounced 'droi')*

BERKELEY: *(A bit more confused)* Eh?

LANDLORD: Droi! Now you was sayin', sir! *(He breathes meaningfully into the BBC man's face)*

BERKELEY: *(Getting the point)* First, I insist on drinks all round.

(In a swirl of activity, they refill their glasses and the atmosphere further relaxes)

LANDLORD: Now, sir. You was askin' about drats and I was about to show 'ee a drattin' pole. Obadiah! *(He calls over one of the besmocked yeomen carrying a pole)* This is Obadiah Smothergoose, our local champion dratter.

OBADIAH: How do?

BERKELEY: Delighted! Is that a drattin' pole?

CRIES OF: Ooh! Aah! Drattin' pole! Best made! Petrified English bog-oak. Show 'im, Obadiah! Bog-oak 'er be.

LANDLORD: Obadiah is a cack hand – keeps his *left* hand low. Show the Lunnon gentleman your drattin' pole.

(Obadiah hefts the long, gaily-coloured pole about in a professional manner – half crouching as he does so)

LANDLORD: Now that's drattin' for you, sir! Lovely loose knees and plenty of flexibility in his lumbar region.

(Obadiah flexes his lumbar)

ALL: Bootiful! Real drattin'!

LANDLORD: Note the drattin' pole – all lovely matured petrified English bog-oak.

CRIES OF: Ah, lovely! Bootiful! Petrified! 'Tis!

LANDLORD: This is the foresight for alignin' the pole. *(He indicates a spring-shaped object on the end of the pole)* This is the hand-guard or Waffle-Banger.

BERKELEY: Waffle . . .? *(Enquiringly)*

LANDLORD: *(Completes it)* . . . Banger! Waffle-Banger. Protects the leadin' drattin' hand at high speed. This is the Nurdle Grip . . .

CRIES OF: Aah! The Nurdle Grip!

BERKELEY: What is it for?

LANDLORD: 'Case of nurdlin'! Naturally! 'Mazin' you didn't know that!

CRIES OF: 'Mazin'! It's for nurdlin', naturally!

BERKELEY: Naturally!

LANDLORD: And finally, *(Proudly)* note his Threep Danglers.

BERKELEY: *(Bristling)* Threep Danglers? Where?

LANDLORD: These. Danglin' down as plain as a pikestaff. *(He indicates three brightly-coloured balls dangling on woven strings)*

OBADIAH: *(Filled with pride)* The wife made them. She's got a marvellous touch with my Threep Danglers.

BERKELEY: Charming! What happens now?

LANDLORD: The runnin'!

BERKELEY: The running?

LANDLORD: Exactly! You're catchin' on fast. But afore the runnin' comes the wettin'.

CRIES OF: Afore the runnin' comes the wettin'.

BERKELEY: Wetting?

LANDLORD: In water. Obadiah first wets his boots in spring water.

BERKELEY: Why?

LANDLORD: For the grip. He must have a good *wet* grip with his boots or he might nurdle.

CRIES OF: Ah! Obadiah might nurdle? Never! Not Obadiah, too much lumbar! Not nurdle – never! *(Some of them are quite vehement)*

LANDLORD: Every dratter has to face facts. There is *always* the danger of nurdlin'. If *you* be afraid you might nurdle, then I say – don't drat.

CHORUS: Aah! Don't drat! Not if you be nurdle-shy.

BERKELEY: Sounds dangerous.

LANDLORD: Oh! Terrible perilous, drattin' be.

BERKELEY: Well, now Obadiah has wetted himself, can we see a running?

LANDLORD: So you shall, sir! So you shall! Ted Mossop will be Lurker.

BERKELEY: Did you say Lurker?

LANDLORD: Aah, Lurker! See! The dratter has to 'ave a Lurker to lurk by the door, ready to open it and let him out for the drat run.

BERKELEY: I see! *(He doesn't but he feels he must say something)*

LANDLORD: Now, Obadiah gives his signals to the Lurker, who replies in the time-honoured manner of his lurkin' forefathers. All right, Obadiah! Let's drat!

OBADIAH: *(Shouting to the Lurker)* Queen Anne's bloomers.

LURKER: *(Tensely at the door)* Henry the Eighth's kneecaps.

OBADIAH: *(Loudly)* Disraeli's bedpan.
LURKER: *(Throwing open the door)* Gladstone's big brown warts.

(With the pub door open Obadiah runs out, holding his dratting pole like a lance. Thunderous applause from all and then deathly silence as the Lurker slams the pub door. Everyone is frozen like statues now listening intently to the sound of the dratting run)

BERKELEY: I say! What?
LANDLORD: *(Fiercely)* Quiet, sir! 'Tis a drat.

(As the tableau of rigid, listening yeomen seems locked into immobility, we hear Obadiah's running footsteps disappearing into the distance. He runs over gravel, then tarmac and pavement, on to sand and finally his footsteps fade into silence. During the running he crashes into and through various obstacles that splinter, crunch and disintegrate – loudly culminating in the distant sound of a huge pane of glass shattering)

LANDLORD: *(Relaxing visibly)* Twenty-two! *(He turns and marks the score on a large blackboard next to Obadiah's name)*
BERKELEY: Was that good?
LANDLORD: Not bad. But at one moment I thought he'd nearly nurdled.
VOICE: Never! Not Obadiah. Too much lumbar, he'm got. Don't 'ee say that 'bout Obadiah!
LANDLORD: *(Placatingly)* I said *nearly* nurdled. Could happen. Even to Obadiah.

(Another dratter has taken Obadiah's place, hefting his slightly different drat pole, but standing reversed with his back to Berkeley)

LANDLORD: This 'n be Hezekiah Trumbleweed. 'E's a southpaw. That's a left-hander.
BERKELEY: How unusual.
LANDLORD: Unique. That's what Hezekiah is – unique. Only left-handed dratter in the county.
BERKELEY: How many dratters are there in all?
LANDLORD: Countin' Obadiah Smothergoose? *(Counts carefully)* Two. Hezekiah's the other one.

(Hezekiah has had a wooden tub filled with a white liquid placed beside him)

BERKELEY: *(Pointing)* That's not water.
LANDLORD: Pig's milk. Hezekiah is an international.

16

(All remove hats. Hezekiah wets his boots in pig's milk and signals the Lurker)

HEZEKIAH: *(Shouting)* Old Mother Reilly's incontinence knickers.
LURKER: Richard the Third's hump.
HEZEKIAH: King William's rupture appliance.
LURKER: King George's codpiece!

(At this last piece of historical information Hezekiah starts his dratting run, with the Lurker whipping the door smartly open and then slamming it shut. Everyone, including Berkeley, freezes into intense listening poses. The sound of Hezekiah's run is subtly different from Obadiah's – a blend of splintering matchboard, skidding sounds, a ricochet and accompanying breaking glass and, as the footsteps die away, a rending crunch of impacted metal – with a sharp cry. Groans from the assembled drat fans)

LANDLORD: I hate sayin' it 'bout Hezekiah, but that were a very near nurdle.

CRIES OF: Aah! Nearly nurdled did Hezekiah. Never thought oid live to see the day. Bloody careless! Man could do himself a mischief like that, aah! Nearly nurdled at the third hazard. Nasty. Very nasty.

LANDLORD: Still, he didn't.

BERKELEY: Didn't what?

LANDLORD: Nurdle. That's what he didn't. There's an old saying in these 'ere parts. So long as 'ee doesn't nurdle, 'ee be on the straight and narrow, loike.

ALL: Aah! *(Hats off)* Keep to the straight and narrow and the Lord protect us from nurdlin'.

LANDLORD *et al.*: Amen.

BERKELEY: Amen, I say. Do you think I could have a go?

LANDLORD: What, sir?

BERKELEY: I'd like to try a running.

CRIES OF: *(In amused amazement)* Ooh! Aah! Well, I'll be nurdled. And 'im nobbut a lad.

LANDLORD: I admire your pluck, sir. Well, boys. *(He addresses the yeomen)* What do 'ee think?

YEOMEN: Aah! Admirable. Very plucky. Spunky lad. Aah, why not 'ave a go, lad?

LANDLORD: 'Ere's a spare pole. *(Berkeley grabs it)* Now, sir, nice loose knees . . .

(Berkeley crouches, bouncing up and down)

LANDLORD: Little more lumbar.

(Berkeley gives a bit more lumbar)

LANDLORD: That's good.

BERKELEY: Shall I use the pig's milk?

LANDLORD: *(Reluctantly)* No, sir!

BERKELEY: *(Already putting one foot towards the water bucket)* The water, then?

LANDLORD: *(Horrified)* Not in Obadiah Smothergoose's water, please!

(Everyone gasps)

BERKELEY: *(Confused)* Sorry.

LANDLORD: You try a nice dry run, sir. Less chance of you nurdlin' on your first drat run. Now I'll give your signals to the Lurker.

BERKELEY: Right!

18

(He tenses for the run, a look of do-or-die determination on his face)

LANDLORD: *(Shouting)* Teddy Roosevelt's spectacles.
LURKER: Queen Mary's toenails.
LANDLORD: Lloyd George's bunions.
LURKER: Kitchener needs you. *(Points to Berkeley)*
LANDLORD: That's you, sir. Away you go!

(With great concentration, the BBC spokesman runs clumsily past the Lurker and through the open door, which slams shut behind him with an ominous clang. Everyone listens in rapt silence as we hear Berkeley's stumbling run over gravel, pavement, grass and muddy terrain, crashing through and past various deadly obstacles, which crunch and disentegrate. Then suddenly there is a cry of despair, the sound of an approaching express train, a tearing skid and a car-crash, followed by a dying scream as Berkeley falls over a cliff into the sea far below. This ends abruptly in a distant splash.

In mute horror the yeomanry remove their hats and stand with bowed heads)

LANDLORD: *(In subdued shock)* Drat me! He nurdled!
CHORUS: Aah! Poor bugger.

Commentators on OBs (Outside Broadcasting) i. the old days of steam radio had to be extraordinarily good ad-libbers. The same applies today in live television though, with the arrival of videotape, editing has become possible and many of the old problems of commentating have disappeared.

Recently on the BBC coverage of the first Columbia shuttle landing, I heard a young commentator struck dumb for words – probably because he was so overcome by the incredible feat of landing the giant glider from outer space. The poor man floundered around like a beached whale. This could never have happened in the old days. Having done live commentary, I know that if you once stop talking you're 'dead'.

DISASTER AT THE NATIONAL GALLERY

How many times have commentators on Royal occasions had to fill in with absolutely nothing happening around them *before* the august personages arrived, or bullshit their way out of the situation when the studio 'came over' to them just *after* the procession had left them in a vacuum of inaction. It was a case of either: 'There's a tremendous air of expectancy and excitement as this huge crowd awaits the arrival of Their Majesties – and any moment now they *will* arrive – and what a beautiful day it is! The sun pouring down on the good-natured swarm of happy spectators, the birds singing in the blossoming trees which line the route, etc, etc' (as the commentator prayed that Their Majesties would get a move on) or it was the other way round: 'I wish you could have been here to see the ecstatic greeting that welcomed Their Majesties as they drove along in the blazing sunshine, with the trees in full blossom above them, the birds singing away, etc, etc' (with a scheduled four minutes to fill in before saying those beautiful words: 'And now, back to the studio').

Richard Dimbleby, the doyen of them all, once filled in a long pause of inactivity in Parliament Square, when Her Majesty had been held up somewhere en route, with a long dissertation on Big Ben starting with the words: 'Loyal, loyal Big Ben booms out the hour of noon' (which it then proceeded to do, completely drowning that wonderful voice).

It is to Richard Dimbleby's memory that I dedicate this sketch.

The imposing front of a great gallery, not necessarily an accurate representation of the actual National, but with an impressive sweep of steps coming down to the pavement. The commentator, Quentin Cobbling, is standing confidently in front of two imposing carved doors which are, at the moment, shut. A large poster is beside one of the great door panels. It reads: PICASSO EXHIBITION, *and is illustrated by one of the master's more obscure weirdos.*

It is late evening one weekend and the great metropolis is relaxed and almost empty. Quentin is going to take the viewers round the Picasso Exhibition personally and give them the benefit of his ignorance.

QUENTIN: Good evening and a warm welcome to the Quentin Cobbling Hour. For the next sixty minutes we are going to go round the great National Gallery to enjoy the delights of Picasso at his most provocative. *(He extends an elegant forefinger and presses the ornate bell-push)* What a fine display of the great master's Catalan talent it is. *(He presses the bell-push a little harder and for a trifle longer and we can hear the distant bell quite clearly)*

QUENTIN: *(Still cool but a touch piqued by the lack of response to his regal summons)* Very soon now we will treat ourselves to those little shivers of ecstatic delight that Picasso-lovers invariably seem to feel in' the presence of his great genius.

(This time he holds down his forefinger for several seconds while the bell frantically buzzes away somewhere in the bowels of the great gallery, but still nothing happens)

QUENTIN: *(Losing some of his pompous composure and knocking on the great door with the fine bronze lion-headed knocker)* Such a unique gathering together of so many of the great artist's masterpieces in one exhibition . . . *(Knocks even louder)* . . . is a rare feast for the art connoisseur and . . .*(He whacks the great door with a couple of resounding thumps from his heel but all is silent within)* . . . we are *so* lucky to be able to partake of this veritable orgy of colour and line, and shape and form – for some of his exquisite little maquettes and *objets trouvés* are here as well.

(Obviously no one is forthcoming and Quentin is scheduled live for a whole hour)

QUENTIN: *(Taking a deep breath)* These great doors I am knocking on . . . *(Knocks hard while yet again the hollow booms echo through the deserted building)* . . . are by the immortal Grinling Gibbons – to whom we owe such a great door debt. *(Kicks them hard in a fit of pique)* They are very solid, a beautiful example of that great door designer's – er – great door design.

(Quentin now realizes what has happened, but he's in full flight and is certainly not going to admit that he's there on the wrong night)

QUENTIN: *(Searching for a way round the problem)* The – er – marble steps that I am standing on are made of marble – as one would expect and are probably not by Grinling Gibbons, but are *(He starts to descend them)* more probably the work of one of the great Victorian staircase designers, who have left us such a glorious legacy of marble steps and imposing stone stairways.

(By this time Quentin, complete with trailing mike, is about to step on to the pavement outside the gallery)

QUENTIN: The pavement I see is *(Examines it closer)* by the London Pavement Ccmpany, whose fine work we take so much for granted, and these railings *(He tries them to see if he can climb over them to peer in through a side window)* are probably by the London Railing Company, which replaced so many of the iron railings in London, which were taken down and used for scrap metal in the Second World War. *(As he examines them, he sees that one section is climbable and is just about to scramble over when he spots something just inside the railings – a pile of bricks and some sand and cement, obviously left there by builders working on the gallery)* Ah! *(He reaches in through the railings and extracts half a brick)* This half-brick is almost certainly a product of the *(Reads it)* London Brick Company, who supply most of the bricks for buildings in our great metropolis . . . *(He hefts it in his hand)* and *(More confidently)* very soon now *(He eyes the large side-window)* we will be inside the National Gallery and well on our way to viewing the glorious Picasso Exhibition.

(Quentin is just about to climb over the railings with his half-brick when the heavy-booted tramp of a policeman's large feet prompt him to hide the brick behind his back – turning with an innocent smile as the 'fuzz' passes ponderously by)

QUENTIN: *(All innocence)* Evening, officer.
FUZZ: Good evening, sir. Lovely evening.
QUENTIN: Indeed! That's what I was about to say myself – a lovely evening.
FUZZ: *(Departing)* Good night, sir.

(As the fuzz's feet plod off into the distance, Quentin nips over the railings with a muttered oath and a ripping sound)

QUENTIN: Christ! Er – *(Recovering himself immediately)* – Jesus Christ has often been the subject of Picasso's work and I *do* believe that we will be seeing some fine examples of these portrayals of the Master by – er – the master of arts – to – er – coin a phrase. *(By this time Quentin is over the railings and is already trying to heave open the window, without success. He peers into the dim interior of the silent gallery)* This window, which is also a fine example of British window making, seems to open on to a side gallery and . . . *(He hurriedly looks left and right to see that the coast is clear)* . . . very soon now we'll be inside the gallery and in a few more minutes we will be able to view the marvellous masterpieces of the great Picasso himself.

(He takes a couple of steps backwards, shades his eyes with his left hand and throws the half-brick through one of the panes of the window. The glass crashes back into the room and he reaches in and releases the catch inside)

QUENTIN: *(Unruffled and obviously pleased with himself)* Yes. Very soon now we will be among that Eldorado of paintings, the Picasso Exhibition. *(He heaves the window open and with much effort struggles over the sill into the darkened gallery beyond)* Obviously by the smell of turpentine and varnish I can safely say that this side gallery is one of those havens of art conservation, the – er – restoration area of the National – famed throughout the world for its fine conservation work on some of the greatest masterpieces known to man.

Yes, I'm right. I can dimly see many unframed canvases and panels stacked against the walls and benches, loaded with brushes and cleaning fluids and – er – *(He absent-mindedly strikes a match to see better)* Ah, indeed, yes, here in this long, high-ceilinged room must be gathered many of the great secrets of art restoration – the brilliant and – er – painstaking work of master craftsmen. Oh, sh – *(He nearly says it as the match burns his fingers and he drops the match-end with a cry of pain)* Ouch! Anyway, I can confidently say that in a very few moments our eyes will be confronted by the greatest collection of Picasso paintings Great Britain has ever seen. *(He coughs as smoke starts drifting lazily upwards from below the window ledge)* If you will follow me!

(He nods to the invisible camera crew, who have been patiently photographing his every move)

QUENTIN: *(Coughing as more smoke rises and the crackling of flames is heard)*

Oh, Gawd! *(He snatches off his jacket and starts beating out the fire)* Oh, sweet Jesus!

(There is an explosion, more smoke billows up and we hear a fire alarm ringing)

QUENTIN: I won't be a moment. Don't go away. I'll . . . Oh, God Almighty!

(He gives up trying to cover up his own monumental stupidity and frantically snatches up a fire extinguisher from the wall and starts playing its hissing froth of foam on to the now raging fire beside him. Sound of fire-engines with bells clanging, police cars with sirens whooping and a skidding heavy truck stopping suddenly. Quentin has now completely disappeared in the smoke. Out of the truck (off screen) comes a trench-coated commentator pulling a trailing microphone. He is obviously American. He positions himself outside the window and peers out front to his camera crew – blowing into his mike to test it)

AMERICAN COMMENTATOR: OK, fellahs! Get a quick, wide shot of the fire and zoom in on me. One, two, *(Blows)* three. OK, you guys. Here we go. *(He takes a deep breath, coughing with the smoke)* Shit! OK – we're on the air. *(He immediately calms down and becomes tensely professional)* Hello, viewers! This is Clyde Quigley reporting for NBC News from London, England. I am standing outside Britain's famed National Gallery, where a four alarm fire is presently threatening this great treasure house of the art world. Is it sabotage? The work, perhaps, of some fanatical terrorist group of ultra-activist militancy? Or is it a natural disaster – due to some careless philistine who . . .? *(Clyde is interrupted by Quentin's paroxysms of coughing)* My God! Some gallant art lover is still inside the great gallery, risking his or *her* life to save some at least of the world's masterpieces.

(Through the window several canvases come flying, one hitting the American. He peers into the smoke, which parts to reveal Quentin, who is nearly passing out from the fumes)

CLYDE: Jesus! Hello there, Quentin! I didn't recognize you for a moment. *(He covers the mike)* Christ, what a fire! What are you doing here?

QUENTIN: *(Between coughs and masterpiece-chucking)* Oh, hello, Clyde. I'm covering the Picasso Exhibition live for the BBC. What are you here for?

CLYDE: I'm covering the disastrous fire that is threatening to destroy Britain's famed National Gallery . . . *(Pauses)* . . . for NBC. *(Realizes he is still on the air, recording a big news item, and suddenly reverts to his dramatic professional voice)* Quentin Cobbling, well-known British broadcaster and art and cookery expert, have you any message of hope for the millions of art lovers all over the world who are watching these tragic scenes – horror struck?

QUENTIN: *(At last panic-stricken)* Yes! Heeeeelp!

The first job I got in the film business was as a 'crowd artiste'. Very few future stars have actually made their way up from the ranks of the crowd to become top names in the cinema. Errol Flynn was one and David Niven was another and one or two girls fought their way out of the 'extra' classification, to win a star on their dressing-room doors.

In the late thirties and after the war, the world of the 'extra' was still a shadowy one of long queues at agents' offices. Very few extras actually made a living at it: most of the 'crowd artistes' had part-time jobs as waiters and waitresses, and their late-night work financed their daytime fantasies as movie actresses and cinema actors in the 'crowds' at Ealing, Shepperton, Pinewood, Denham, Shepherd's Bush and Elstree, where the film studios were located.

THE FILM EXTRA OF THE CENTURY

Although the film extra has no lines to speak and only becomes a 'character' by virtue of his or her costume, there still exists the strange convention that an extra plays a definite part in a crowd scene. For example, 'I'm playing a down-and-out in my next picture'; 'I was a burly sailor in my last picture'; 'I played a badly wounded civilian in the Blitz'. The character becomes identified with the costume and with whatever the assistant director tells the crowd artiste to do, such as: 'When I shout action – fall down' (though this technically could be regarded as a stunt).

In the few pictures in which I appeared as 'A young RAF cadet sitting down (while on leave)', 'A French dandy standing up in a tumbril', and even 'A young sailor in anti-flash gear holding a heavy shell', I believed I was being an actor, which I suppose I was.

I met some marvellous characters in the world of the crowd artiste and a few villains, and sometimes I was appalled at the way some jumped-up assistant directors (who are really glorified call-boys and 'gophers') treated these good-natured and gentle people. In their way, extras are dreamers, hiring out their fantasies with tolerance and enthusiasm, and I am not being patronizing when I state as a fact that you can't make a 'big' film without them. They also possess or acquire a marvellous sense of humour which, in Britain's brutal climate, they certainly need.

I wrote this sketch for my dear old friend Peter Sellers. It was one of his favourites.

The stage of a huge movie theatre during the Annual Awards Dinner. It could be in Hollywood or the West End of London, Cannes, or Rome. The atmosphere is unmistakable – that wide-mouthed fixed-smiling air of a Lucretia Borgia dinner with its 'who gets it next' sense of anticipation. Whether the presentation is the Oscar, the Emmy, the Golden Bear or the Silver Tit doesn't matter: the film and television industry is giving itself a well-deserved pat on the back.

Behind the inevitable pulpit type of desk stands the Presenter, a self-important actor chosen specifically for his ability to speak lines which haven't already been written for him.

However, as an aide-memoire, the Presenter either has an 'auto-cue', a neat device that reflects his lines on to a glass screen in front of each of the television cameras he faces, or he uses 'idiot boards', which are large pieces of white card with the words written by hand on them. When I have to use them I prefer their other name, 'cue cards'.

Either way he must be able to manoeuvre between the lines and to pick up the cues when and where needed.

PRESENTER: *(Breezily)* So much for the Best Supported . . . *(Crowd laughs)* . . . I'm sorry, I'll read that again, Best *Supporting* Actress of the Year. Now we come to a new category in our annual award, a special classification for those artistes in our great industry, who up till now have never received the recognition long over-due for their talents. This is to be a special award to the film extra of the year – given to one of that great body of talented actors and actresses who grace the crowd scenes of our epic motion-pictures. *(His sincerity is brittle as spun glass, but the vibrant emotion in his voice is well-rehearsed and unmistakable)* For this one occasion only, the first time such an award has ever been presented, the category reads, *(He puts on reading glasses over his contact lenses)* 'For outstanding contributions to the movie industry over the past sixty years.' *(He removes his glasses with a perfected flourish)* The winner is Mr Charles Crumpet, Film Extra of This Century.

(Crowd enthusiasm. Onto the stage comes Charlie Crumpet, an aged actor-laddie with a moth-eaten astrakhan collar on the overcoat draped over the shoulders of his evening dress, which is green with age)

CHARLIE: *(His quavering, throaty voice overcome with emotion)* Thank you. Thank you. I don't know what to say.

PRESENTER: Well! Up to now, in all your sixty years on the screen, you haven't said very much. So don't worry, Charlie, we all know you and many of us here tonight have worked with you.

CHARLIE: *(Emboldened by this tribute)* Indeed, sir! I remember so well, working with you in *The Albanian Connection*. I played the role of a dissolute Albanian organ-grinder asleep in a doorway.

PRESENTER: *(Lying boldly)* Of course! So you did.

CHARLIE: It was a two-day job. Quite a demanding role. The monkey suffered from diarrhoea and I was covered with . . .

PRESENTER: *(Leaping in)* A red blanket! I remember distinctly. You were wrapped in a red blanket in the doorway.

CHARLIE: Was I? I can't remember.

PRESENTER: Yes, indeed, Charlie. Now, your career started way back in the early days of motion pictures, with D. W. Griffiths. How did you get your first part with the great Griffiths?

CHARLIE: Well, I was spotted by one of Mr D. W. Griffiths' talent scouts.

PRESENTER: In a picture?

CHARLIE: No, on a picture-postcard of Brighton beach. I happened to be sunbathing at the time when the picture was taken.

PRESENTER: *(Genuinely surprised)* Amazing! To pick just one person out of that whole crowd on the beach at Brighton, England.

CHARLIE: Well, actually, it was February and I was the only one on the beach. I was a hardy all-year-round bather when I was young and I was *(He modestly lowers his voice)* beautifully built. This must have caught the talent-spotter's eye. He was as gay as a goose you know, queer as a coot, bent as a corkscrew, a raving . . .

PRESENTER: *(Hurriedly interrupting)* Quite so, a lucky break. What motion pictures did you make for D. W. Griffiths?

CHARLIE: *Intolerance*, of course. I played several parts in that – a Babylonian panther trainer: I still bear the claw marks; then I played a drowning Philistine and, lastly, a dying Sadducee. Three days work altogether.

PRESENTER: Fascinating!

CHARLIE: *(Unstoppable now)* Then I was in *Birth of a Nation*, in which I played a badly wounded Confederate colonel, a drunken Yankee carpet-bagger, a sinister hooded member of the Ku-Klux-Klan and, finally, a runaway slave for which, of course, I had to wear heavy make-up.

PRESENTER: *(Seizing the opportunity to get in)* Then came the First World War. Did you enlist?

CHARLIE: In a way, yes. I was in uniform for Mr D. W. Griffiths' epic recruiting masterpiece *Bullets Over the Somme* but, sadly, it was never shown.

PRESENTER: Why not?

CHARLIE: By the time we'd finished making the motion picture, the war was over. However, I made five hundred dollars from that one part. I played a young British lieutenant who was hit by a German shell.

PRESENTER: That seems like a lot of money for a small part.

CHARLIE: Ah, but it was a real German shell. The money was by way of compensation. *(Before the Presenter can get going again, Charlie continues)* Then I struck a bad patch. I was out of work for fifteen years. This was due partly to my war-wounds and partly to my having gained the compensation only after a long legal battle. Companies don't forget things like that, you know.

PRESENTER: *(Hurriedly)* Well, that's show business. When did you start to get work again?

CHARLIE: With Mr Cecil B. de Mille, another great gentleman of the silver screen, in *The Ten Commandments*. I got a small speaking part, as a starving beggar outside the gates of Jerusalem. I said *(He goes into the full character bit)* I'm starving, I'm starving. *(His voice breaks)* I'm starving!

PRESENTER: *(Impressed)* That was very good.

CHARLIE: Well, I *was* starving. Anyway, Mr Cecil B. de Mille noticed me – just before I fell down in a dead faint – and he gave me work.

PRESENTER: *(Sonorously)* A great director!

CHARLIE: Oh yes! I worked for Mr de Mille on a number of motion pictures. In *Samson and Delilah* I was a Philistine, hit by Mr Victor Mature with the jawbone of an ass. He *broke* my jaw! Then in the remake of *The Ten Commandments* I was the Egyptian character who was nearly drowned in the Red Sea, and in *David and Bathsheba* I was the warrior smitten on the forehead by the boy David. He fractured my skull. An accident, of course, as he was aiming at Goliath at the time.

PRESENTER: Did Mr de Mille have you in *all* his pictures?

CHARLIE: Mr de Mille always asked for me by name. He'd say: 'I must have Charlie in my next motion picture.'

PRESENTER: *(Surprised)* He asked for you by your Christian name, Mr Crumpet?

CHARLIE: In that context he could hardly have used my surname! Yes, indeed. Mr de Mille always had me in his motion pictures. I can't think why. *(Pauses thoughtfully)* I'd never done him any harm.

PRESENTER: I understand that you are now starting a new career? Is that so, Charlie?

CHARLIE: Well, in a way, yes. I have sustained so many injuries in my various roles as a crowd artiste or, as we say nowadays, as a 'non-speaking' actor in motion pictures, that I have finally been accepted by the union.

PRESENTER: But surely you have been a member of Actors' Equity for years?

CHARLIE: Yes, of course. I meant another union, the Stuntmen's Union.

PRESENTER: You surprise me. At your age it's incredible.

CHARLIE: But true. In my next motion picture I shall be the first eighty-year-old man to fall off a ninety-foot tower – or is it the first ninety-year-old man to fall off an eighty-foot tower? I'm afraid my memory is not what it was.

PRESENTER: *(Handing Charlie a multiple Oscar)* Before you go, Charlie, have you any message for your undoubted millions of film fans out there?

CHARLIE: Yes. How kind. I'd just like to say that Miss Lillian Gish and I are just good friends. *(He pauses rather sadly)* We couldn't very well be anything else.

(Thunderous applause and cheers as Charlie gets a standing ovation)

These are a particularly fascinating species who habitually suffer from acute verbal diarrhoea. In common with 'race callers' who give an inarticulate running stream of inaccurate information during horse races, most sports commentators over-describe the action.

During the last Olympics, when several nations declined to take part at the Moscow Stadium, these splendid people, the commentators, outdid themselves. As most of the information displayed electronically on the gigantic bulletin board was in Russian they redoubled their efforts to explain for the viewers and listeners what was going on. Most of this rapid-fire bombardment of descriptive prose was wildly enthusiastic and often totally inaccurate, but the commentators obviously enjoyed themselves. One British genius described a United Kingdom runner who was lagging far behind the field as: 'Coming in confidently and superbly fit – a gallant sixteenth!'

Yet another sad and ineffective effort was described as 'A new record for his Walthamstow club', or something equally delightful.

I've enjoyed them all, from the melodious Oxford-bred tones of Howard Marshall, the great pre-war cricket commentator, to the countryman 'burrs' of John Arlott and David Vine. The commentators' pro-British partisanship is as evident as their love affair with their own sonorous vocal chords. They are as British as Stilton cheese.

These next pieces are dedicated to their marvellously bigoted and totally unsportsmanlike bias in favour of their country's sportsmen. Long may they and those that come after them continue to delude the great British sporting public!

THE SKI-JUMP

Stock film of a typical 'hairy' ski jump on a sound picture for radio with an excited background atmosphere. Garbled voice over Tannoy and full echo-effect: 'The first entry is from Soviet Russia: Vladimir Cockalotovitch, Number Twelve.'

COMMENTATOR: *(In the hushed and vibrant voice that accompanies a dangerous athletic feat)* And next to go is the Russian, Cockalotovitch – a newcomer to Olympic ski-jumping – but I believe well-qualified by by Soviet standards. A bit of a dark horse, this youngster has still to prove himself. And there he goes! Oh! Not too confident a run – knees a little too close together for comfort and elbows a shade too loose . . . *(Ski-running effects stop. Crowd gasps)* Not too good a take-off and his ankles look too tight for a good jump. Not a bad effort, but he could fall far short of the Chipping Sodbury champion's fine jump yesterday. I spoke to him when he regained consciousness and he was quite confident that both legs will set nicely. Ah! *(Crowd gasps and thunderous applause)* Yes! A bit rocky on the landing but Cockalotovitch just got away with it. A very lucky young man.

TANNOY: A new world and Soviet record of 99.9 metres for Vladimir Cockalotovitch.

(Crowd ecstasy)

COMMENTATOR: As I said, a lucky break there for the Soviet ski-jumper. He could so easily have not made it. The wind changed at *just* the right moment.

TANNOY: *(Another echo double wobble effort)* The next skier is Pierre de Wigan for France.

(Cheers)

COMMENTATOR: Another chancy entry for this great Olympic event that has me, for one, puzzled. Pierre de Wigan is experienced and as overall European Victor Skidorum *quite* good in his own way. The winner of thirty-nine world titles, he may well be over the hill when competing against our own reigning Giggleswick champion, Fred Grockle, who did so brilliantly for the Worcestershire semi-finals on the grass slopes of the Wrekin last winter. Ah! There he goes – once again a dodgy start to what could well be a disastrous jump. *(Ski-slide effects stop abruptly. Crowd gasps)* Oh dear! A badly timed take-off there – elbows a little too far forward and his knees much too straight. He's stretching it – yes! He's stretching it. *(Ski-slide sound renews. Crowd cries out and applauds)* What a bit of Gallic luck! La bonne chance, as the frogs say.

(Thunderous applause and whistles)

TANNOY: A new French and European record for France: 99.999 metres.
(Gallic shrieks of joy)

COMMENTATOR: Well, we'll see who laughs last.

(Crowd's thin applause)

COMMENTATOR: *(With terrific enthusiasm)* It's Fred Grockle's turn to show the Olympic Committee what the British team can do.

TANNOY: *(Warbling as wobbly as ever)* Number Thirteen for the United Kingdom, Fred Grockle.

(Crowd is totally uninterested but that doesn't deter the commentator)

COMMENTATOR: Yes, it's Fred Grockle. A great favourite with the crowd – looking fit and bronzed after his successful operation and considerably lighter than last year – as well as four inches shorter. And there he goes! What a superb run. A picture of compact power. Everything tucked well down – giving minimum wind resistance.

(Ski-slide effects stop. Crowd gasps)

35

COMMENTATOR: *(Deliriously)* What a take-off! Superb. Fred's grand windmilling style and pumping knee action are unique – a true poetry of frenzied activity as he cunningly sways from side to side – revolving gracefully in mid-air. And what a jump! Up, up he goes. *(Crowd gasps in disbelief)* Yes! There he goes. An unbelievable jump. Certainly. *(Uncertainly)* What a fantastic leap! Yes, indeed, quite incredible! *(Even more uncertainly)* Absolutely amazing! *(Crowd amazement)* The jump of the century! Bloody hell!

(Disappearing cry of 'Heelp, Jesus!' as Fred disappears into the wild blue yonder)

COMMENTATOR: *(Finally deciding to pass the buck)* Well – er – back to Michael Bentine in the London studio.

MB: Thank you, Jeremy. Back here at Broadcasting House we are eagerly awaiting the results of the Olympic ski-jump and . . .

(MB's voice is interrupted by a wailing scream rapidly approaching, followed by the sound of a wall collapsing and window glass shattering as Fred lands in the studio)

MB: Well done, Fred Grockle! A new Olympic record and an undoubted gold medal – posthumously.

THE SHOW JUMPER

The following sketch became an RCA record and keeps on appearing on radio programmes. To my amazement, HRH Prince Charles told me it was a special family favourite. As a matter of fact, when his ADC asked me if I could get the Prince of Wales a copy, I thought it was for use as evidence – and later I had an odd dream in which I finished up in the Bloody Tower.

The sound scene is typical of Olympia as the venue of indoor show-jumping, rather than the exterior perspective of the great county fairs. The usual buzz of crowd noises is interrupted by the Tannoy announcement.

TANNOY: *(A wobbly echo)* And now for the jump-off in the final Salmon and Gluckstein Cup. Number 27, Carmelita, ridden by Colonel Spellotti for Italy.

(A thin uninterested spatter of British applause greets the announcement as Colonel

Spellotti faultlessly rides the beautiful mare Carmelita into the show-ring. Sound of horse cantering.

COMMENTATOR: *(Being British he can't bring himself to speak disparagingly of the horse, but he makes up for this by cutting Colonel Spellotti down to size)* Colonel Spellotti rides in the typical loose style of the Italian show jumpers. Not too much control over his lively little mare, Carmelita, who is showing herself to be very much in command. There he goes up to the first fence and . . . Oh! A bad take-off, forefeet much too close to the fence and . . . *(Crowd: light gasp)* . . . he just clears it by a mere . . . *(Pause)* . . . three feet. Had the wind changed Spellotti would have been in very real trouble.

(Horse canters up to second fence)

COMMENTATOR: There he goes for the second fence – *not* his day. Bad judgement. Colonel Spellotti allowing Carmelita far too much of her own way. Oh my! He's just made it, though. Carmelita saved the day for her rider and managed to clear the triple bar by a scant two feet – very chancy! Indeed! *(Crowd: thin interest)* Coming up to the third fence now, the Colonel seems to be having a hard time making up his mind about when to give Carmelita her head. Oh, he's muffed it again. *(Sound of faultless take-off and landing)* Gosh! What a lucky chap the Colonel is. The wind must have changed at the crucial moment and just carried the horse and rider over the top bar – scraping it narrowly by only a foot or so clearance.

TANNOY: A clear round and the record time of 43 seconds for the jump-off in the final by Colonel Spellotti, riding Carmelita for Italy.

(The Colonel canters his superb mare out of the arena. Very thin applause by the disappointed crowd, who were hoping the Italian might break his neck)

TANNOY: *(Greatly excited and with even more echo effect than usual)* Yes! As you can hear by the enthusiastic reception from the crowd, it's Her Royal Highness riding Kinky for Great Britain. *(Crowd goes ape)*

COMMENTATOR: *(Sycophantically over-enthusiastic)* And, of course, that roar of ecstatic welcome was for Her Royal Highness riding Kinky – such a popular favourite here since she was retired from the United Dairies.

(Sound effect of a three-legged horse with a loose sphincter – a tracheostomy, asthmatic and obviously of great age. Its hooves are erratic in their lolloping progress. Crowd cheers)

COMMENTATOR: What a picture they make! Horse and rider literally welded into one. A perfect picture of Haut Ecole at its best – sometimes it's even a little difficult to tell which is which. There they go – coming up to the first fence – perfect position for take-off and . . . *(Crash of falling poles as Kinky breasts the first jump)* Oh, what shocking bad luck! Kinky just tipped the top bar with her nose – a tiny bit overtrained perhaps, but that's the luck of the game.

(The wheezing wreck of the near-knackered beast approaches the second fence – summoning up every gasping effort to get off the ground)

COMMENTATOR: What a sight they are! The graceful young Royal rider and the show-wise experienced mount, her belly close to the ground and nostrils well distended, with that funny little back kick of the legs as she jumps, and – er – Kinky doesn't look too bad either. Ah, there's the take-off. Perfect. Absolutely perfect positioning of Kinky's forelegs. Oh!

(Splintering crunch and muttered feminine: 'Christ' as Kinky demolishes jump number two. Crowd gasp of horror)

COMMENTATOR: Oh, what appalling bad luck! It was the same last month in Spain – probably the grass – the rich clover-filled grass of Britain can play tricks with a highly sensitive thoroughbred like Kinky. *(Loud blast of horsey 'wind' punctuates the commentator's remarks)* Yes. I thought so – it was quite enough to tip the balance against them, and Kinky just failed to clear the fence. Ah! *(Pace of Kinky changes slightly to one of a stumbling canter. Crowd cheers her on)* Just coming up to the water jump – and Kinky has got both ears well laid back for this one. There's grace and beauty for you. Oh! *(Terrific skid. Crowd gasps amazement)* Good heavens, I can't believe it. Kinky's *refused*! But . . . yes! I'm sure of it. Her Royal Highness has *accepted*!

(Sound of running booted Royal feet – an effort and a big splash as HRH descends in a flying belly flop below the surface of the water jump. The crowd goes bananas)

COMMENTATOR: *(Beside himself with ingratiating patriotic fervour)* What a brilliant swimmer Her Royal Highness is! Well up to Olympic standard. What superb style! Marvellous!

(Cries of 'Help' from the half-drowned future heir to the throne – give or take a couple of others)

My childhood and adolescence were greatly influenced by the cinema – at first, in the late twenties, by the silent films of the Buster Keaton-Charlie Chaplin era and then in the thirties by the Laurel and Hardy 'talkies' (they had also made magnificent silent three reelers).

Musicals such as *Rio Rita*, with Bert Wheeler and Robert Woolsey, and *42nd Street*, with Dick Powell and Ruby Keeler, vied for my favours with Johnny Weismuller's

and Maureen O'Sullivan's Tarzan epics. I loved the romance and adventure of various silent and talking versions of *Robin Hood*, *The Black Pirate* and *The Three Musketeers*, with stars ranging from Douglas Fairbanks, Sr, to Errol Flynn and Cornel Wilde. I cheered Sabu and Douglas Fairbanks, Jr, and hissed Basil Rathbone (except as Sherlock Holmes) and Conrad Veidt.

What an era that was! Only a shadow of its glory remains today in the TV re-runs of old movies. From the moment the lights went down in those grubby little cinemas of my youth in Folkestone, the flickering magic took over and I became a wondering part of the absurd adventure stories projected on to that silvery screen.

One of my all-time favourites was the genre of films made about Africa, with gallant white hunters and virginal solar-topeed heroines, with veils wrapped round their absurd headgear.

I now realize how much of it was shot on the studio back lot and how much grainy 16 mm background film was actually made on location in Africa. I believed every single frame and I only found out the truth about Africa when I went there after the war.

The faithful M'Gombo – the archetypal intrepid gun-bearer, who is invariably tossed high above the charging elephant while protecting his 'Bwana' – is a myth. No self-respecting African would be found dead in such a situation.

The white hunters are real enough, but often short and tubby, or lanky and myopic like my splendid brother-in-law George who, on his own admission, is as 'brave as a mouse', which is probably why he is still alive and still hunting.

This sketch was written after seeing *Mogambo* with Clark Gable in the role of the great white hunter saving Grace Kelly, who looked luscious in a tight khaki shirt and skirted boots.

Like Deborah Kerr in the Stewart Granger version of *King Solomon's Mines*, Miss Kelly blindly tripped over everything from snakes to panthers and even fell in front of an evidently very short-sighted 'white' rhino, who kept shedding his coat of latex emulsion in clouds of white dust.

This piece is a tribute to all the African 'men of iron' who slaughtered the game for the movie camera and all the dim-sighted ingenuous beauties who succumbed to their strong, silent charms.

Alan Watermain, the Great White Big Game Hunter, is strolling happily alone through the dense undergrowth of the rain-forest. He is smoking his battered old pipe and all six feet two inches of him is blissfully at ease with his natural environment. Dressed in his 'white-hunter's' safari hat with a leopard-skin headband and his worn, sweat-stained khaki drill bush-shirt, and trousers tucked into jungle boots, Alan, with his tanned leathery face, is about as macho as you can get. The sounds of the jungle echo around him in a savage chorus. His peaceful thoughts are interrupted by a voice nearby.

VOICE: Mr Watermain? Mr Watermain? Where are you?

WATERMAIN: *(Calls)* Lady Cynthia, I'm over here – this way. To your right. Follow my voice.

(Into the jungle clearing comes Lady Cynthia Belting, the brand-new, far-too-young, wife of Lord Belting, a rich and elderly peer of the realm)

LADY CYNTHIA: Thank heaven I've found you, Mr Watermain! *(She bats her long false eyelashes at him and straightens her topee, which has got caught up on a bush)* What a lovely evening it is!

WATERMAIN: *(Who is not very experienced with beautiful young aristocrats or rather the young wives of elderly aristocrats)* Lady Cynthia, you shouldn't be out here alone. The jungle may look beautiful, but it's really no place for a woman – alone. Where is your husband?

LADY CYNTHIA: *(Archly)* Oh! I left him asleep back at the camp. He's got a touch of gout. Too much port. He's all right, but he's not young and needs lots of sleep.

WATERMAIN: He shouldn't have let you come out on your own. It's far too dangerous.

LADY CYNTHIA: *(Moving right in on her target, until her tightly upthrust breasts almost touch him)* Oh, that's all right. I feel so safe with you, Mr Watermain. You're so *(She touches his massive biceps and then strokes them)* strong. So terribly strong. *(She lifts her lovely lips towards Watermain's down-turned face, trembling with eagerness to be kissed – so that even Water-main feels the sexual tension and automatically responds, gently holding the lovely safari-outfitted Lady in his mighty arms)*

WATERMAIN: Lady Cynthia, you are a lovely vibrant young woman here alone with me, a lonely man in the beauty of the jungle evening . . .*(He pauses alertly)*

LADY CYNTHIA: *(Swaying in towards his chest waiting to be crushed against the hunter and smothered in his macho kisses)* Yes, Alan.

WATERMAIN: *(Suddenly rigid)* Don't move, Lady Cynthia! As you value your life. Don't move a muscle! It's a deadly snealth spider. One bite from those terrible fangs and you're dead. Don't move, my dear!

(As he speaks, the hunter slowly draws a .45 revolver from its holster and gently raises it in line with Lady Cynthia's horror-stricken head. Then, as the large hairy arachnid slides down its web to attack its prey, Watermain fires a thunderous blast right next to Lady Cynthia's ear and blows the deadly spider to bits)

LADY CYNTHIA: *(Screaming)* Oh, my God, Alan! *(She hurls herself at him and he tries to comfort her)* What a terrible beast! Oh, Alan. Hold me close! I'm terrified. *(Her genuinely frightened face is now turned helplessly to him; her lips are parted in desire, touched with fear; the hunter is just about to kiss her passionately)*

WATERMAIN: *(Cuddling her)* Calm yourself, my dear. There, there. It's all over. You're quite safe.

LADY CYNTHIA: *(Recovering and quivering with the 'hots')* Oh, Alan. My brave, brave Alan! I owe you my life. I'm yours. Take me.

WATERMAIN: Lady Cynthia, I'm a man and you're a woman and I . . . *(Once again he's suddenly all attention as a huge snake slowly sways down towards them from the tree above)* Don't move, my dear! If life is dear to you, my dear, don't move! Lady Cynthia, it's a giant python – the most deadly snake in the jungle. *(Once again Lady Cynthia is rigid with terror, her lovely eyes bulging with shock and horror)*

WATERMAIN: *(Gently, between clenched teeth)* Don't move! Keep absolutely still! Rigid as an iron bar! *(The hunter sneaks up his huge revolver and belts two shots into the python, which falls in seemingly endless coils to the ground – the gun totally deafening Lady Cynthia's other ear)*

LADY CYNTHIA: *(Exploding out of her terror-stricken silence)* Oh, my God, Alan! Oh, hold me, hold me! It nearly got me. Oh God, Alan! I was nearly killed. That ghastly creature.

WATERMAIN: *(All sweet words and comforting arms – his passion mounting as the half-hysterical beauty forces herself against his manly chest and equally manly*

43

lower half) Steady on, old girl! A miss is as good as a mile. Here, rest against this tree for a moment and catch your breath.

(He leans the willing girl back against a substantial tree and leans on her himself, pressing against her thrusting body and about to kiss her passionately)

WATERMAIN: *(Huskily)* Oh, Lady Cynthia! If only you knew how I've dreamed of this moment! How I've longed for it.

LADY CYNTHIA: *(Breathlessly standing on tiptoe)* Oh, yes, Alan! Yes, at last. My strong, wonderful Alan. Tell me you love me.

WATERMAIN: I have much more to say to you, Lady Cynthia, my beautiful darling.

LADY CYNTHIA: What, Alan? What? Tell me! What is in your heart?

WATERMAIN: *(Suddenly alert again as the two hairy arms of a hidden giant gorilla encircle the trunk of the tree, searching for Lady Cynthia)* Don't move, Lady

Cynthia! It's an enormous mountain gorilla. He can tear you to pieces with two fingers. Don't move, my darling – not a muscle! Not an inch!

(Lady Cynthia goes rigid as the great hairy hands creep over her body. She is past movement and paralysed with horror)

WATERMAIN: Stay absolutely still, my darling! *(Watermain draws his revolver and 'bangs' off two of the remaining three rounds of .45 ammunition into the great hidden beast. With a dying roar it sinks down invisibly behind the tree, its huge hands straying down Lady Cynthia's curves, in a last voluptuous gorilla's farewell)*

LADY CYNTHIA: *(Losing control)* Oh, Alan! That was horrible. Oh Christ. That was awful. Oh God, how I hate this bloody jungle and this stupid bloody safari! I must have been stark staring mad to leave the bloody West End and come on this mad cock-eyed bleedin' farce. Oh Christ, how I hate bloody Africa. Oh Gawd! How I hate every bleedin' thing about it! Africa? Christ, you can keep the whole bleedin' stinking shit-heap and stuff it. Oh Gawd! What a bleedin' life! Get me back to civilization, you bloody muscle-bound moron –or I'll tell my bloody berk of a husband that you tried to rape me. You bleedin' chauvinist pig! *(All through this tirade of terrified invective Alan Watermain has been trying to get a word in edgewise, to stop the flow of rancid hatred, as Lady Cynthia's carefully-cultivated Oxford accent disintegrates into her native Cockney. As she rants on, he falls silent. Lady Cynthia is pacing wildly up and down in her fury and now has her back to the hunter)*

WATERMAIN: *(Quietly)* Don't move, Lady Cynthia!

(Once again the terror-stricken girl stands stock-still, speechless at last. Watermain draws his trusty .45 and aims it at her ladyship's back – firing his last round into her gorgeous body. Lady Cynthia is blown flat on to her lovely boobs. Watermain sighs, then whistling a cheerful tune, he steps over the beautiful corpse and exits, humming happily to himself in the restored peace of his beloved jungle)

Of all the many and varied accents and dialects that have held my fascinated attention over the years, one of my favourites is the 'Indian' accent. Not of course the Hollywood version: 'Long knives come from across river – yellow hair, Custer, chief of white eyes – speak with forked tongue,' but rather, the genuine subcontinental variety – the Pakistani and the Sikh, the Sri Lankan and the 'African' Indian. Their accents are sheer joy.

THE SUITCASE SHOP

All have subtle differences in the musical rendition of versions of the English language, and Peter Sellers captured their cadences beautifully in *The Millionairess*.

I am not a racist, being the possessor of a large number of ethnic genes (Spanish, Moorish, Flemish, Inca, Dutch and Anglo-Saxon) and I consider myself an 'International'. However, I believe that if the misguided self-appointed moralists are allowed to clamp down on the 'ethnic' jokes and the gentle humour of dialects then they will be virtually screwing down the safety valve of an overcrowded multi-racial society.

This doesn't mean that I accept bitter 'anti-minority' sarcasm as genuine ethnic humour, which is often devised and presented by the minorities themselves: the Jewish sense of humour is, of course, world famous and very self-deprecating, so is the Scottish sense of fun. But I do believe that without true ethnically-based humour much of our sense of humanity will be lost.

I am proud that among the Indian communities in Britain I have had a large and approving audience for some years, yet in my children's programmes *(Potty Time)* I often used the gentle cadences of the accepted Indian accent (sometimes called the 'Bombay' accent).

This sketch is typical of the many fond tributes I have given to my many friends in Britain's Indian communities.

A corner of a small shop specializing in Travel Goods. It is located in a provincial town in Britain. The proud owner-manager is Mr Singh, a splendidly moustached and bearded member of his ancient religion, handsomely turbaned, urbane and smiling. His spotless overall is the badge of his deep knowledge of the luggage trade. The door-bell tinkles and a customer enters, a small precise man in a raincoat, muffler and 'flat hat' (a nondescript checked cap)

MR SINGH: *(Brightly, in Sikh accent and intonation)* Good morning, sir. A lovely day.

FLAT HAT: It's raining.

MR SINGH: Lovely for de garden. Vot can I do for you, sir?

FLAT HAT: *(In a flat voice)* I want a trunk, a good, solid, waterproof trunk.

MR SINGH: *(Warming to his task)* And you've come to de right place, sir. A vaterproof trunk. You are travelling far? By sea, perhaps?

FLAT HAT: No. I'm not going by sea. I'm going by *air* – to South America.

MR SINGH: *(Professionally alert)* Then, sir, may I recommend you reconsider your requirements? A vaterproof trunk such as you probably are thinking of vill cost a fortune to send by *air*, especially if you are going a long vay. Vot about an expanding suitcase? *(He indicates one, picking it up and placing it on the counter)* Like this one. Quality guaranteed and qvite light.

FLAT HAT: No, mate. I've got my old suitcase. That's not what I'm looking for. *(Slowly)* I want a nice big waterproof trunk, good and strong.

MR SINGH: *(Sighing for his customer's stubborn folly)* Very vell, sir. You are de customer and ve have an old Sikh expression vich says, 'De customer is alvays right.' A trunk it shall be. Vot colour do you like? Brown, green, blue, aluminium?

FLAT HAT: It doesn't matter. The trunk's not for me. It's for the wife.

MR SINGH: *(Suddenly seeing the light)* Ah! De trunk is not for you. But is for your vife.

FLAT HAT: That's right, mate. I'm going by air. The wife's going by sea.

MR SINGH: How romantic! A nice long sea voyage for your dear vife, and you, sir, are going on ahead, flying to a new life in a new land, to prepare de vay for your bride. I did the same thing. Coming here from Bombay to Birmingham.

FLAT HAT: Oh? *(He's not very bright)* Yes, the wife's going by sea – to Australia – the *long* way round.

MR SINGH: *(Not at first comprehending)* I vould still recommend that your vife vould be better off with a fine, strong, hand-crafted leather suitcase – almost as good as a trunk, but lighter – made of finest leather hides by Sikh craftsmen. *(He leans over the counter, his bright eyes sparkling with humour)* Vot ve call in Bombay *(Deliberately)* a 'Hide and Sikh' suitcase. *(The joke goes over Flat Hat's head)* Yes! Vell, never mind.

FLAT HAT: No, mate. The wife would never get in that. She needs a big waterproof trunk. To travel in.

MR SINGH: *(Not quite certain that he has heard aright)* Your vife? I'm sorry,

sir. *(He giggles)* I thought for one moment that you said your vife needed a vaterproof trunk to travel in.

FLAT HAT: *(Who is a gentle psychopath)* That's right, mate. The wife's going to Australia *in* the trunk. It's me what's going to South America in a plane.

MR SINGH: *(Feeling that he is losing the polo ball)* Vait a minute. You mean that your vife is going to Australia by boat – as a *stowaway*? I cannot be a party to dat.

FLAT HAT: Oh, no, mate. That would be against the law. No. The wife's going to Australia by boat all right. But the legal way. I'm paying for the freight. Proper. Nothing illegal.

MR SINGH: *(With dawning realization)* You mean to say that your vife is *inside* de trunk – and it's legal?

FLAT HAT: That's it, mate. The wife will be nice and snug inside the trunk. She'll be all right, mate. Don't you worry yourself.

MR SINGH: *(Panicking)* But I *do* vorry myself. Vot have you done?

FLAT HAT: *(Leaning over the counter and speaking confidentially)* I *done* her in. So you see why it's got to be a trunk, mate?

MR SINGH: *(Horrified – almost in a whisper)* You *done* her in?

FLAT HAT: S'right, mate. I done her in. Proper!

MR SINGH: *(His control snapping)* Oh, my goodness gracious. You. You come in to my shop – and you tell me dat you vant a vaterproof trunk and you tell me dat you vant it to put your vife inside to send to Australia – by boat and you *done* her in. Oh, vot a calamity! Vot a calamity!

(As Mr Singh does his nut in blind rising panic, Flat Hat pulls out a photograph and shows it to him)

FLAT HAT: 'Ere, 'old on a minute, mate, look at that. That's a picture of the wife.

MR SINGH: *(Automatically taking it from him in mid-tirade and slowly focusing on it)* How dare you, sir! Come into my beautiful, respectable shop and try to make me a travel accessory after de fact. I'm going to call de police – de fuzz – I'm going to have you arrested, sir, for causing a disturbance of de peace and quiet of my shop. I . . . I – er – vait a minute! *(His face is a study)* Dis is your vife? *(His voice conveys total disbelief)*

FLAT HAT: Yes. That's her. That's the wife.

MR SINGH: *(All sympathy for his unfortunate customer)* My God! You poor infidel. *(Brightly)* Now vot you need, sir, is one of our very best first quality, all aluminium, guaranteed vaterproof steamer trunk. I can recommend it with a clear conscience. Guaranteed personally by me, Ram Singh, to never leak. Dat's vot you vant, sir. A good reliable hand-made piece of Bombay craftsmanship. Best price.

(We fade out as Mr Singh extols the virtues of his splendid product)

My own confidence in treaties took a hard knock when Adolf Hitler referred to the 'Peace in our Time' document that he had signed with Neville Chamberlain as: 'A scrap of paper'. Nevertheless, Heads of State still set much store by such 'scraps of paper' and threaten each other with ever more deadly and more horrifying weaponry until such documents are signed.

THE TREATY (THE SHEIK-DOWN)

Pacts of non-aggression – treaties of arms-limitation and other weighty examples of the international lawyers' craft – are still eagerly sought after and reluctantly ratified. It all provides an enormous amount of work for the big international law firms and senior civil servants but, unless it is backed up by the sincere goodwill of the signatories, the whole exercise is worthless.

Only if the peoples of this world can learn to trust each other will any of this unbelievably expensive mumbo-jumbo become a valid reality.

I respectfully dedicate this sketch to the professional diplomats who have to bend over backwards to heal the rifts made between nations by the arrogance of politicians.

A huge, expensively decorated tent, set somewhere in the great Arabian desert. Seated among a gigantic pile of gaily-coloured cushions is the mighty Sheik Abdul al Bull En Shallah, an oil potentate of venerable appearance and incredible age. His vizier, Achmed al Halava, is at his right hand to see that the Sheik gets his full ration of petro dollars and behind him two eunuchs are plying their great ostrich-feather fans. Beside him a couple of nautch girls are on hand to carry out his every whim.

The mighty Sheik's noble beard flows in a white waterfall from his nut-brown, wizened countenance to below his waist and by its gentle trembling it is obvious that the sheik has the shakes, due to too many nautch girls and too much Arabian Expresso. Arabic music of a peculiarly unappealing discordancy is being played.

Enter a grovelling major domo, prostrating himself before the 'Presence'

GROVELLER: Oh, mighty one! Son of the sun, moon and stars!

Emperor of the great oasis of Suleiman the Magnificent! Prince of the . . . !

VIZIER: Yes, yes. Never mind de commercial. Get on with it.

GROVELLER: *(Rising to his feet and salaaming)* Oh, Great Sheik! Her Britannic Majesty's representative, His Excellency de British Ambassador.

(The dignified and imposing figure of the British sovereign's representative enters attired in full tropical regalia – spotless white-duck uniform heavy with medals, red sash and the order of St George, narrow white trousers, a sword, and a plumed solar-topee – a splendid vision of Western imperialist decadence)

GROVELLER: *(Announcing him)* Sir Osbert Main-Waring!

SIR OSBERT MANNERING: Sir Osbert Mannering. Your Serene Highness. *(He gives a stiff courtly bow. His white-gloved hand holds a large treaty, rolled up and sealed)*

SHEIK: *(Muttering something and waving a trembling hand)* Bul bul muk muk ma balla balla, insha allah.

(The Vizier translates airily and with supreme confidence in his command of the English language)

VIZIER: *(Haughtily)* His Serene Highness, son of de sun, moon and stars etcetera, etcetera greets Her Britannic Majesty's humble representative and bids you welcome, Sir Osbert.

(Sheik burbles on inarticulately)

VIZIER: His Serene Highness further extends de usual hospitalities and customary extravagant offers of anything and everything that His Serenity possesses – with de usual proviso that you will not take advantage of any of it whatsoever!

SIR OSBERT: *(Drawing himself up to his full five feet five inches)* And in reciprocation I bring her Britannic Majesty's warmest greetings and sincere wishes for His Serene Highness's continued good health and Her Majesty's sympathetic condolences on His Serene Highness's recent great loss.

VIZIER: Indeed a tragedy. It was His Serene Highness's favourite racing camel, you know.

SIR OSBERT: *(Sympathetically)* A great sadness. Her Britannic Majesty had a similar inconsolable loss, when Kinky – Her Majesty's parade horse – passed away last year during Trooping the Colour.

VIZIER: *(Sighing)* Ah, well, Sir Osbert, we must bear our losses with fortitude.

SIR OSBERT: *(Holding up the treaty)* Perhaps, then, we can discuss the renewal of the existing oil treaty between our two great countries?

VIZIER: Insha allah! *(He raises his beringed hands to heaven with a well-rehearsed shrug of his shoulders)*

(The Sheik mutters some more Arabic wisdom)

SHEIK: Alwallah wallah dhobi mak-mak impshi gulli-gulli mala-mala baksheesh.

VIZIER: Before we discuss de treaty, we must, of course, extend to you, our distinguished guest, the courtesy of our traditional Bedouin hospitality. *(He claps his hands and a nautch girl hurries forward with a brass tray, on which are two small glasses of some steaming green liquid)*

VIZIER: *(To diplomat)* Please be seated, Your Excellency. Here, beside His Serene Highness.

(The British Ambassador sinks down with practised professional grace and some difficulty, with both his sword and hat in his free hand. The extreme compressability of the large cushions comes as a surprise – in fact, he really does sink down among them, finishing up slightly below the level of his venerable host)

VIZIER: *(Offering the Ambassador a green 'steamer', with a gesture)* First, please drink a glass of muk-muk. It's our custom. Our ceremonial beverage.

(The Sheik takes one glass and the Ambassador the other)

SHEIK: *(Muttering into his beard and waving the glass about in what is obviously a toast)* Wallah wallah barrakat.
VIZIER: To our two great nations and de Treaty!
AMBASSADOR: *(Eyeing the glass with some alarm)* To our two great nations and the Treaty!

(The Sheik drinks it down in one gulp, spilling some into his beard where it lies green and smoking. (Note: we had a small wire basket under the beard with 'dry ice' in it and as the warm green liquid hit it, it 'smoked' splendidly.) The Ambassador obviously dislikes the beverage intensely but drinks it all down.)

SIR OSBERT: *(With an effort)* Delicious. Now – with regard to the renewal of the Treaty – my government feels that a more reasonable figure per barrel would be . . .
VIZIER: *(Interrupting mercilessly)* We have not yet completed de required formalities according to Bedouin protocol. Sir Osbert, it's your turn with de next toast. *(Claps hands and another nautch girl arrives with two much larger glasses of the bubbling green liquid)*
SIR OSBERT: *(Reluctantly taking one)* I propose a toast to the continuing health of His Serene Highness and the amicable relations between our two great rulers.

(The Vizier translates for the Sheik and the elderly potentate shakes with approval)

SHEIK: Ay wallah akbar bar Coca-Cola insha allah!
VIZIER: De old twit couldn't agree more.
SIR OSBERT: *(Reacts in horror)* I say, steady on, Your Excellency.
VIZIER: Don't distress yourself, Your Excellency. De old goat can't speak a blind word of English. Not a bloody syllable. *(He smiles*

ingratiatingly at his shaking master) Can you? You ancient bag of impotent bones.

(The Sheik warmly returns these implied pleasantries, chortling away happily to himself and goosing the odd nautch girl)

NAUTCH GIRL: Ooh!

VIZIER: *(Smiling servilely)* Horny old sod!

SIR OSBERT: *(Having downed half the repellent-looking liquid with some difficulty)* Quite delightful. What is muk-muk exactly, Your Excellency?

(The Vizier grins and whispers in the Ambassador's ear – to his growing consternation and horror)

SIR OSBERT: Good Lord! *(He looks at his nearly empty glass, which is still bubbling away)* Is it? *(He shuts his eyes tightly and drinks it with gallant determination)* Ugh! Is it, by jove? *(He turns to the Vizier)* You must have an awful lot of camels.

VIZIER: Millions of de bloody things! Keep telling old 'four eyes' here dat we need tanks and planes and guns and all de other advantages of Western civilization – and all we get are more bloody camels – he's a bloody camel freak.

SIR OSBERT: Ah yes, well! Your Excellency, perhaps we can come to some arrangement. We in Britain produce some of the finest weaponry in the civilized world – perhaps a large part of our oil treaty payments could be in arms.

VIZIER: *(Sharply)* Not on your Nelly Bligh! You give us petro dollars and we will buy what arms we want. None of your second-hand war-surplus crap for us. Thank you very much indeed.

SIR OSBERT: *(A bit taken aback, but game to the last)* I meant, of course, our very latest arms, all with a one-year guarantee and full service warranty. *(Persuasively)* On very advantageous terms – fifty million pounds down and the rest on agreed extended payments.

VIZIER: *(With a short, nasty laugh)* On de never-never? I should bloody well coco! Never. Cash only. None of your HP sauce.

SHEIK: *(Breaking in)* Ah, mish mish mallah mallah willy wally muk-muk!

VIZIER: *(Raising his eyes to heaven)* Oh God! Droopy drawers wants some more muk-muk. *(Claps his hands)* Sorry, Sir Osbert, you'll have to oblige. Drink up and smile.

(The nautch girl hurries on with – this time – two giant glasses of the bubbling green muk-muk)

55

SIR OSBERT: *(Brokenly)* Oh, my God! *(He smiles bravely)* Ah well, here's to crime. Down the hatch. *(He is partly overcome by the neo-hallucinogenic qualities of the virulent beverage, and partly by his failure to get the terms that his mission requires)* Your Serene Highness. Long may you reign in majesty, Your Majesty.

(As the Vizier translates, the Ambassador tries to drink the liquid, which spills down out of the huge glass and turns his spotless uniform into a virulent mouldy green, while his medals start to sizzle. Note: we used Alka-Seltzer tablets – the large ones – covered in watercolour silver paint. They worked beautifully, but you must use hot water)

VIZIER: *(Fascinated by this sizzling medal phenomenon)* Watch it, Your Excellency. Your medals are melting.

(The Ambassador has spilled a lot of the liquid into his hat, which is upside down in his lap, partly filling it with the green camel-tea)

VIZIER: *(Brightly)* Well, now! Drinks are over. What did you want to ask His Serene Highness, old Slobberchops here?

(Sir Osbert starts to speak, then, overcome with the Arab diuretic, he hurriedly whispers into the Vizier's ear)

VIZIER: *(Comprehending immediately)* Naturally! *(He points)* De first on de left and behind de second rock on de right!

(Sir Osbert scrambles up with difficulty from his encushioned position and bows, putting on his solar topee and covering himself in a further green shower as the Vizier stops him for an instant)

VIZIER: Not behind de *first* rock. Dat's de ladies!

ANNOUNCER: The only way out of a recession is for everyone to pull their weight and do their best to sell overseas the export goods that their country produces. British sporting goods are a good bet, but you must find the right markets. For example, not everyone in Middle Europe plays cricket, especially not in Transylvania.

CRICKET ON THE CONTINENT

(Sound of a storm: rain, thunder, lightning. Carriage on cobblestones. One pair of feet across wet cobbles)

VOICE: Keep the change, cabbie!
(Lightning/thunder. A horse gallops off with a rattling carriage behind it. Door opens, creaking, and slams shut, cutting off the storm outside. Rustic Transylvanian conversation stops abruptly)

SALESMAN: *(Very British)* Good evening! Evening, landlord! Good evening all! *(Silence)*

LANDLORD: Dra? Dra?

SALESMAN: Do you speak English? I'm a British sporting goods salesman. Have you a room for the night? For night? Nacht? My name's Wally Purgis.

(Groans at the word 'Nacht' and Wally Purgis)

SUSPICIOUS CUSTOMERS: Nacht? Dra! Walpurgis. Nacht? *(Shudders)* Walpurgisnacht! *(Lightning)*

LANDLORD: Britisher? Du Britisher?

WALLY: Yes, that's right. Do *you* speak English?

LANDLORD: Noo. Nie English. Moment. Meine Dictionarish Transylvanian–English!

(Sound of heavy book being taken up and plonked down on to a table and dust blown off)

WALLY: Oh good! English–Transylvanian dictionary! *(Blows more dust; leafs through pages)* Splendid! Let's see now. Cricket? Cricket? Oh dear! Doesn't seem to have it. *(To landlord)* You know – er – *cricket* – c r i c k e t – er – bat. Ball! Umpire! Umpire!

LANDLORD: *(Terrified)* Vampire? Bat! Ah – batsk! Vampire – batsk. Walpurgis – nacht! *(Terrific thunder and lightning)*

(Cowering customers' groans, Transylvanian praying, etc.)

WALLY: Yes. Umpires. Bats. Wicket. Wicket!

LANDLORD: Wicked! Wicked! *(Groans)*

WALLY: I'm here to sell! Sell! *(Loudly)* British cricket goods – bats – balls – wickets – pads! *(Sound of goods being dropped out of his bag on to a table-top)* Like these!

CUSTOMERS: Aah! Ooh!

LANDLORD: *(Picking up something wooden)* Is vats? Is vats? *(Bangs wicket stump on table)*

WALLY: Stump. Wicket stump. Let's see. *(Rifles through dictionary)* Stump – no. Stave – pointed stick. Stake, that's it! Wicket stake!

LANDLORD: *(Seeing the light)* Aah! Stakei für wicked! *(Stake is shown to others, who agree. Much Transylvanian chatter)*

ALL: Stakei für wicked – vampire! Batsk! Güt! Güt! *(Demonstrate stake)*

WALLY: I thought you'd like them. *(Customers agree)* Well made. British made. From finest willow. Like this bat.

LANDLORD: *(Taking bat and banging stump with it)* Aah! Bat banger! Güt! Güt! Banger stake! Wicked batsk! Vampire! *(Demonstrates)*

ALL: Vampire! *(Lightning)* Wicked! *Güt* stake! *Stake 'em hertz!* Güt!

WALLY: Yes. And these are pads. Pads – protection. Gloves – protection.

LANDLORD: Protection. Güt. Protection.

ALL: Protection. Walpurgis! Wal purgis! Nacht! Vampires! Walpurgis!

WALLY: That's the name. Call me Wal!

LANDLORD: *(Picks up something else)* Vas da? Vas da? Wal?

WALLY: *(Embarrassed)* The box – b o x. *(Looks it up in dictionary)* Box – coffin!

LANDLORD: Coffin? *(Surprised)* Kleine vampire! Britisher vampire kleine?

ALL: *(Amazed)* Hier grosser! Muche grosser! Da! Hier grosser! Kolossal!

WALLY: It's protection for your – er – well, your – er – matrimonial prospects. Protection!

ALL: Aah! Protection! Güt! Güt!

(Burst of thunder, flash of lightning, and the door crashes open. All terrified. Wolf howls)

DRACULA: Good evening. What a lovely night!

WALLY: Oh splendid! Someone speaks English. My name's Wally Purgis.

DRACULA: How interesting. Quite a coincidence. Tonight of all nights!

WALLY: I'm a cricket goods salesman – also tennis, squash and croquet but our rule is no blood sports.

DRACULA: Pity! Perhaps you would honour me by being my guest? At my castle. I am Count Dracula.

WALLY: How kind! These people here seemed a bit confused. Perhaps you would be interested in our latest cricketing books and manuals. This one is especially good – guaranteed to turn you into a first class bat.

DRACULA: I can hardly wait. Come! *(Crash of thunder and lightning)*

WALLY: Haven't I seen you somewhere before – in the *Daily Mirror*?

DRACULA: Impossible! You'd never see me in the mirror. Dead or alive!

(Door slams with a crash, maniacal laughter and storm effects into musical tag)

There is a popular misconception that life in the countryside is peaceful and quiet.

I remember many years ago going down to Dorset to stay at my wife's family home near Sherborne. This was a thirteenth-century manor house dating from the reign of King John, with additions by succeeding owners, ranging from early Elizabethan to late Lego.

Asleep in King John's room (which has a wall-frieze preserved by the National Trust) I was jerked horrifically awake by the most blood-curdling noise I have ever heard. I lay shivering with terror and bathed in a cold muck-sweat when the ghastly alien sound again screeched forth.

'Peacock!' muttered my wife sleepily. 'It's just a bloody peacock! Go to sleep!'

That weekend I wrote the following.

A COTTAGE IN THE COUNTRY

The dark, gloomy interior of a typical British country cottage with low twisted oak beams and an inglenook fireplace. It is furnished with reproduction furniture of the 'nicky-nigh-noo' period, a mixture of fake Stuart, phoney Queen Anne and neo-Georgian formica.

There is a tomb-like silence which is broken by the rattling of a key in the front door. After some effort, the creaking nail-studded door screeches open. Three people stumble cautiously into the gloomy parlour. They are the house agent, a local 'shrewdy' cashing in on the current back-to-the-land craze among the naive 'Townees' who don't know any better, and an innocently eager young couple, both longing to be convinced that this crumbling rural ruin is to be their 'Cottage in the Country'.

HOUSE AGENT: Well, here she is – Ambrosia Cottage, a lovely little country retreat for you poor over-stressed city folk. Bootiful isn't she?

HUSBAND: *(Enthusiastically)* Delightful! It's so . . . *(He searches for an appropriate word)* . . . so cottagey!

AGENT: Aah! You've hit it, sir. That's what this little gem is. Cottagey.

WIFE: *(Slightly more cautious)* It's a bit gloomy.

AGENT: *(Sharply)* Well, naturally. It's been shut up for some toime. Last owner had to sell it for reasons of health.

HUSBAND: What was wrong with him?

AGENT: He died. *(Hastily)* Not here, of course. In the local cottage hospital. It's not haunted nor nuttin' loike that!

HUSBAND: *(Disappointed)* Oh, we don't mind a ghost, you know.

WIFE: *(Timidly)* So long as it's nice and friendly.

AGENT: Oh, I'm sure that if there *is* a ghost hereabouts it'll be roight friendly. Oh yes, now I come to think about 'un, I did hear tell that the cottage were loively.

HUSBAND: Loively?

AGENT: Loively, meanin' not empty, as you might say.

WIFE: You did say that the ghost, if there is one, is friendly?

AGENT: *(Hurriedly)* Oh aah! *Cuddly*, you moight use the word. Warm and friendly and most amiable. A lovely charming old world presence.

HUSBAND: Whose ghost might it be?

AGENT: *(Lying cheerfully)* Well, it moight be old Mrs Gollop, the widow-woman who was wronged by the wicked squoire, Mad Murgatroyd. Or on t' other hand it moight be the pretty little milkmaid Leticia Bollweevil, who was taken advantage of by the Squoire's potty grandson, who was not 'zactly, as they say in these 'ere parts. But I'm sure they're friendly folk. After all, you didn't do 'em no harm.

WIFE: *(Shivering)* But it *is* a bit gloomy.

AGENT: *(Hurriedly)* Ah! That's all part of its rustic air of peace and quiet. You'll find it a big change after Lunnon! I'll just switch on the loight! *(He presses a switch and we hear a distant motor grind into action. The lights flicker and come on)* Now, that's better. Noice and cosy.

HUSBAND: *(As the noise increases)* What's that?

AGENT: Oh, that? That's just the generator startin' up. Most economical, too. You're not on the mains service 'ere, you know. You need a generator for your loight and all.

(A second sound starts up – a whooshing, sucking sound, with a slight mechanical wheeze and groan built in. The generator has settled down into a steady thumping rhythm)

WIFE: What on earth is that?

AGENT: *(Slightly raising his voice)* Water pump! Comes on automatically, when the generator starts. As oi said, you're not on the mains 'ere. The old well has got a built-in ram-pump – very reliable machinery – put in by the widow Gollop after 'er husband passed on.

HUSBAND: How did he die?

AGENT: Fell down the well. The machinery is a great improvement. A mod con, you moight say.

(*A blast of air shoots out of a grilled opening, blowing dust and debris across the parlour, accompanied by a full-blooded roaring sound like a huge fan with bent blades*)

AGENT: (*Raising his voice still higher*) The heating system – a force-fed hot-air blast, which circulates round the cottage. Very much appreciated when you're snowed up in winter. Kept old Gaffer Cocklecarrot aloive for three days when he were cut off 'ere in the blizzard of '58.

HUSBAND: Really! Saved his life?

AGENT: No. He died of starvation. It were two weeks afore we could get the snow-plough to 'im. But you'll be 'avin' a freezer put in, won't 'ee? There's the fridge Old Mother Cackling put in.

(The grinding scream of a rusty electric motor slowly adds to the cacophony of ear-splitting sound which is now vibrating through the cottage, violently shaking everything)

AGENT: *(Loudly)* Ah! It's still in good order. You'll be all right for food, then.

HUSBAND: *(Shouting over the racket)* Any more generators or other service machinery?

AGENT: *(Proudly)* The dishwasher, of course. *(He switches it on and the general level of chaotic sound pollution gains yet another original mixture of tortured metal, loose bearings and vibrating drives)*

AGENT: *(Yelling)* Very handy. Your wife will appreciate not having to wash up.

HUSBAND: *(Half-deaf with the ear-drum-shattering mechanical chorus that is now bringing down plaster from the low, dusty ceiling)* What did you say?

AGENT: *(As plates start to loosen on the Queen Anne dresser and fall one by one, crashing in pieces on the hard floor)* I said *(Yelling)* the wife will find the dishwasher handy. Save 'er a bundle of housework.

HUSBAND: *(Shouting as loudly as he can)* I can't hear you!

AGENT: *(Over the noise of the vibrating banisters of the short flight of stairs loosening themselves and jumping about in their sockets)* It's so convenient. *(Screaming into the husband's ear)* So handy!

(The banister supports fall out of their holes and crash to the floor. The pictures shake themselves loose from the walls and the Queen Anne dresser topples over, as a huge cloud of soot shoots out of the inglenook fireplace)

AGENT: *(Choking and shrieking above the deafening destruction)* You'll find it a nice change after Lunnon!

When television writers of soap operas are seized by writer's block they usually rework an earlier favourite script episode into an offering for one of the current hospital sagas. With very little alteration except the change of setting, a husband/wife/lover triangle can be redressed into a doctor/head nurse/house-surgeon drama. If need be, and as the current TV fashion dictates, the doctor can be male or female, black, white or any other colour, the head-nurse a transsexual and the house-surgeon an alien from outer space.

THE HOSPITAL SYNDROME

Modern hospital dramas, after the first episodes, seldom reflect real life in their story lines, their only claim to authenticity being confined to the use of medical terminology in referring to the patients' conditions. Memorizing some of the more complex medical terms has driven many a television actor to drink.

A real 'hospital drama' is much more like this.

The casualty ward of a big city hospital. Several examination cubicles are curtained off. A pretty nurse is passing by a row of depressed-looking outpatients. One of them, a middle-aged man in overalls, who has obviously been waiting for hours, stops her.

OVERALLS: Excuse me, nurse. *(He is holding his shoulder and is evidently in pain)* I'm sorry to trouble you, but it's me shoulder. It's giving me real jip.

NURSE: *(Professionally)* I'm sorry, but the doctors are very busy. You'll just have to wait your turn. All the examination cubicles are full.

(At that moment, a doctor comes out of a cubicle where he has been trying on a suit)

DOCTOR: *(To nurse)* I think I'll take this suit. It fits nicely and only the trousers need shortening a bit.

NURSE: *(All smiles)* Right, doctor. I'll tell dad to take 'em up a bit. *(She takes the suit and walks out)*

OVERALLS: *(Seizing the opportunity, grabs the young doctor)* Excuse me, doctor. Me shoulder is 'urtin' somefink chronic. I fell orf me ladder and . . .

DOCTOR: *(Indignantly)* Have you seen the staff nurse?

OVERALLS: *(Indicating the departed angel of mercy)* I told 'er. She told me to wait till the doctor was free.

DOCTOR: Nurse Williams was *off* duty. We're so busy I haven't even got time to go out and get a suit for the Medical Rag Ball. She gave up *off-duty* time to help me out. There's dedication for you!

OVERALLS: Oh, I'm quite sure, doctor. But it's me shoulder. *(He is obviously having trouble with it)* Can't you do somefink?

DOCTOR: *(Relenting)* Oh, very well. *(He indicates the empty cubicle)* Go in there and get your clothes off.

OVERALLS: All of 'em?

DOCTOR: Naturally. I've got to examine you, haven't I?

OVERALLS: 'Course. *(He makes to enter the cubicle)* But it's me shoulder. I fell orf me ladder.

DOCTOR: You may have other injuries. Take off your clothes. *(He goes to run the curtain round the cubicle and the plastic curtain comes off its track)* Oh blast! It's happened again. *(Calls)* Nurse! Nurse! Damn, never a bloody nurse around when you really need one.

(Another young doctor is passing by and stops)

SECOND DOCTOR: What's wrong, Edward?

DR EDWARD: Damn thing has malfunctioned. Can you assist, Godfrey?

DR GODFREY: Certainly. *(He examines the curtain-track with an ophthalmoscope)* These conditions can be very tricky. I remember we had an outbreak like this in Casualty at St Mary's about two years ago.

OVERALLS: Could you look at me shoulder, doctor? I fell orf me ladder. It don't 'arf 'urt.

DR GODFREY: Can't you see I'm in consultation? Get your clothes off. One of us will attend to you in a few minutes. *(Another nurse passes)* Nurse, get the patient's particulars.

(The nurse takes out her pen and writes on a clipboard)

NURSE: Name?

OVERALLS: Arfur. Arfur Jones.

NURSE: Age?

OVERALLS: Forty-eight.

NURSE: Address?

OVERALLS: Peabody Building, East 'am Palace Road. 'Ere, nurse, can you give me somefink for me shoulder? It's 'urtin' somefink chronic.

NURSE: I'm not a doctor. I can't give medication. Get your clothes off.

OVERALLS: I can't. Not till the curtain's fixed.

(The two doctors are now working hard on the curtain, which stubbornly refuses to go back on to its track. A passing specialist, in full consultant's gear, consisting of black jacket, grey waistcoat and black pin-stripe trousers, gold-rimmed half-moon glasses, etc., stops)

CONSULTANT: Ah, gentlemen. Trouble, I see. Can I be of any assistance?

(The two young doctors are very deferential)

DR EDWARD: Oh, Sir Charles. How kind of you.

DR GODFREY: We're most grateful.

SIR CHARLES: *(Pontifically)* I remember a similar case at St Mary's about two years ago. Quite an epidemic, really. *(He puts on an ortholaryngologist's forehead mirror and uses a tongue-depressor to adjust the curtain track)*

OVERALLS: *(Desperately)* Excuse me, doctor! *(He touches Sir Charles, who draws back as though Overalls has the scrofula)*

DR EDWARD: *(Horrified)* Steady on! Sir Charles is a Specialist. I'll deal with you later. Get your clothes off.

DR GODFREY: Bloody sauce. You'd think he was a private patient.

SIR CHARLES: *(To Overalls)* Get your clothes off, man. One of my assistants will examine you. *(Turns back to the real problem)* Now, gentlemen. I think I have a preliminary diagnosis. Yes. The prognosis is . . . *good!* There seems to me to be a mechanical problem, some trauma, localized in this superior posterior area here.

(While Dr Edward and Dr Godfrey grovellingly agree with the great man's diagnosis, a cleaner enters, sweeping out the casualty cubicles. He notices that Overalls is in pain)

CLEANER: 'Ere. What's the matter, mate?

OVERALLS: *(Miserably)* It's me bloody shoulder, mate. Fell orf me ladder. Don't 'arf 'urt, mate. Excruciatin' it is.

CLEANER: *(Putting down his broom)* Let's 'ave a look-see, mate. *(Holds Overall's arm gently but firmly and runs his expert finger over the shoulder)*

OVERALLS: *(Wincing)* Cor! Steady, mate.

CLEANER: *(Sympathetically)* 'Urts there, does it? I thought so. You dislocated it. We get a lot of that 'ere. 'Appens all the time. I'll soon put that right. Brace yourself, mate.

(The cleaner skilfully applies the correct pressure to Overalls' arm and with a loud click the shoulder goes back into place)

OVERALLS: *(Much relieved)* Cor, mate! You done it. A bloody miracle, mate. *(He rubs his restored limb)* Ooh! That don't 'arf feel better. Thanks a lot.

CLEANER: *(Cheerfully)* Shakes you up a bit, don't it, mate? *(He reaches inside his overalls and takes out a notebook and pencil, sucks the end of the pencil and scribbles a note)* Tell you what, mate. *(He tears off the note and hands it to Overalls)* Nip up to the canteen and give this note to Mabel. She'll give you a nice cup of tea and a piece of pie. You'll be as right as rain. *(Overalls goes to leave)* Oh, if you get any more trouble, pop in tomorrow – same time. I'll 'ave another go. Make it eleven o'clock.

(Overalls goes off to get his 'char and wad' and the cleaner sweeps around the consultants and his two minions, who are still completely engrossed in the curtain syndrome)

The reluctance of the British to communicate with each other is legendary. It is also true.

As a family we lived in many different houses in Britain and the least time taken by our new neighbours before they would speak to us was three months. Only in the North of England do neighbours actually welcome the new tenants and arrive on the doorstep with hot tea and cakes as an introduction. However, when communication is finally established in Britain, the interchange of information is like a dam bursting.

CONVERSATION PIECE

In Richmond we finally got to know our next-door neighbour, who turned out to be a funeral-furnisher. He was a large, cherry-cheeked, jolly man who beamed good will in the Pickwickian way. During a bitterly cold winter, he would lean over the garden fence. 'Terrible weather,' he'd say with a radiant smile. 'They're dropping like flies.'

This piece of 'True Brit' is a tribute to the United Kingdom's silent majority, the rail commuters of the London suburbs.

The compartment of the 8.15 a.m. commuter train from Surbiton is empty except for one bowler-hatted, black-jacketed and pin-stripe-trousered city businessman. He is reading The Times. *Normally the train would be crowded, but it is a public holiday and only the dedicated (or the self-employed) are travelling to work. The train starts to grind its way out of the station and running footsteps indicate that another lone traveller is trying to catch the 8.15. A carriage door opens and slams shut, and the compartment door slides open to admit another city businessman, somewhat out of breath. He plumps himself down on the seat opposite the other traveller and, while still struggling to catch his breath, opens the* Daily Telegraph.

The train picks up speed and rattles its creaking way up the line. The first traveller lowers his paper and leans forward.

FIRST TRAVELLER: I say! Forgive my saying so, but you nearly missed the train this morning.
SECOND TRAVELLER: *(Who can't believe his ears)* Er – yes. I suppose I did. *(He thinks for a moment)* Er! Excuse me being a bit forward, but do you

know . . . *(Pause)* . . . that's the first time *ever* that you've spoken to me on this train.

FIRST TRAVELLER: *(Thoughtfully)* I say! I'm terribly sorry. I don't know what came over me. *(Pause)* By the way, how long have we been travelling together on this train?

SECOND TRAVELLER: Twenty years.

FIRST TRAVELLER: Good Lord! Really?

SECOND TRAVELLER: Yes. Twenty years today. I remember because it was the day after I came back from my honeymoon that I started my new job and travelled up on this train for the first time.

FIRST TRAVELLER: Well, I'm damned. What a small world. I've been married for twenty years myself.

SECOND TRAVELLER: 'Strordinary. All those years and we've only just started talking to each other.

FIRST TRAVELLER: Strange coincidence. I hope you don't mind my asking but where were you married?

SECOND TRAVELLER: Locally. At the church on the hill – St Mark's? *(Vaguely)* No, not St Mark's. Er . . .*(He searches for the name)*

FIRST TRAVELLER: *(Helpfully)* St Spencer's?

SECOND TRAVELLER: No. St . . . Oh, dash it . . .

(They both suddenly brighten up and speak simultaneously)

BOTH: St Michael's!

SECOND TRAVELLER: That's the one. St Michael's. Be forgetting my own name next. *(He chuckles)* Were you married locally, too?

FIRST TRAVELLER: Yes, indeed! Same church. What was the name of the vicar? Harry Something?

SECOND TRAVELLER: Quilby? Dolby? Beetly?

FIRST TRAVELLER: Mudby? Godby? Cragby? Name like that . . . Bagby?

SECOND TRAVELLER: *(Remembering)* I know, Hazeltine! Harry Hazeltine.

FIRST TRAVELLER: That's the man. Very old chap. Very short-sighted. Deaf as a post. Dear old Harry Hazeltine – killed climbing the Matterhorn.

SECOND TRAVELLER: That's Harry all right! Keen type! I remember saying that Harry Hazeltine was getting past it to my wife on our honeymoon. It was at St Mawes.

FIRST TRAVELLER: *(Startled)* St Mawes – Cornwall?

SECOND TRAVELLER: Yes. *(Thought dawning)* Don't tell me you spent your honeymoon there? Well, well!

(The First Traveller nods assent)

FIRST TRAVELLER: How odd. We stayed at the Twisted Swan.
SECOND TRAVELLER: So did we. 'Strordinary!
FIRST TRAVELLER: Which month were you there?
SECOND TRAVELLER: Beginning of June.
FIRST TRAVELLER: We were there at the end of June. Oh my!

(There is a short pause while they both 'hum' and 'ha' their surprise)

FIRST TRAVELLER: You always get on the train at Surbiton. Do you live there?
SECOND TRAVELLER: No. I live half way between Esher and Surbiton, but I like to walk down across the common. With my season ticket I can use either station.
FIRST TRAVELLER: We must live pretty close to each other.
SECOND TRAVELLER: Well, I live in Elm Park Avenue and that's . . .
FIRST TRAVELLER: *(Interrupting)* Elm Park Avenue? Good Lord!
SECOND TRAVELLER: *(Amazed)* You don't mean?
FIRST TRAVELLER: Yes, I live in Elm Park Avenue, too.
SECOND TRAVELLER: Well, I'm blowed. Which number?
FIRST TRAVELLER: Number Seven.
SECOND TRAVELLER: Number Eleven?
FIRST TRAVELLER: No. Number Seven.
SECOND TRAVELLER: *(Bewildered)* But *I* live at Number Seven!
FIRST TRAVELLER: No, no. Number Seven. The house with the pink flamingo by the rock pool.
SECOND TRAVELLER: *(Almost speechless)* And the fishing gnome beside it.
FIRST TRAVELLER: *(Amazed)* Blimey! *(Long pause)* What time do you get up in the morning?
SECOND TRAVELLER: Six-thirty. I always was an early riser. Then I go for an early morning jog – get back at seven-fifteen for breakfast.
FIRST TRAVELLER: I always get up at six-thirty-five, shower and breakfast and leave the house by seven-ten. I like to walk the long way round to Surbiton.

(They both digest this information)

FIRST TRAVELLER: Which side of the bed do you sleep on?
SECOND TRAVELLER: The left. And you?
FIRST TRAVELLER: I sleep on the right.
BOTH: *(Simultaneously)* What's the name of your wife?

BOTH: *(Again simultaneously)* Margaret.

(They both subside in deep shock, sitting stunned on their rock-hard seats. There is a long pause while the 8.15 clatters its way to Waterloo. Then they both recover at the same time, determined to display their British sang-froid*)*

FIRST TRAVELLER: Well! One thing's certain.
SECOND TRAVELLER: What's that?
FIRST TRAVELLER: We both married a very remarkable woman.

(They both grunt and once more bury their heads in their spread newspapers)

There is an alternative ending to this piece:

FIRST TRAVELLER: Well! Two things are certain.
SECOND TRAVELLER: What's that?
FIRST TRAVELLER: We both married a very remarkable woman and . . .
   (Pause) . . . it's a lucky thing for Harry Hazeltine that he was killed on
   the Matterhorn.

(They both nod and continue reading their newspapers)

In a world where people distrust each other, it is fortunate that one language (English) has become the international language of the airways. This was brought home to me forcibly when I visited a control tower at a Scottish international airport and heard a broad Glaswegian air traffic controller talking down a Pakistani pilot to a blind landing. The conditions were nearly nil-visibility and the jet airliner from the subcontinent was practically out of fuel. Somehow they understood each other. Would that international conferences managed to do so! This piece shows how much we trust each other.

FREEDOM OF THE AIRWAYS

A modern airport building recently constructed in the late-Lego style. Sounds of great jetliners arriving and departing are mixed with distant announcements that start with: 'Here is an important announcement', are then distorted by the jet noise into incomprehensible gobble-de-gook, and finish with 'immediately!'

A heavy door closes, shutting off the noise, and the sound perspective becomes that of a crowded conference room. A gavel thumps down on its wooden block and a dominant voice takes command of the meeting.

AMERICAN EXECUTIVE: I am delighted to say that we have now completed the formal arrangements for the opening of our new international New York to Moscow Airway.

(Murmurs of approbation in American and Russian, and applause. Glasses are clinked and potato chips crunched)

AMERICAN: *(Warmly)* The inaugural Moscow-New York flight will take place, I understand, on May first – our spring holiday – and the first Tupolev airliner from Soviet Russia will be met by a courtesy flight of F-16 interceptor fighters and escorted all the way from mid-Atlantic, to cross the east coast of the United States at this point here. *(Sound of a pointer being slapped down on a large wall-chart)* The coastline of Maine at this point of landfall is rugged and deserted, but an excellent navigational aid for exactly determining the position are the clearly sited anti-aircraft coastal defences consisting of our new and deadly ground-to-air Bald Eagle missiles.

The Russian jetliner will then proceed down the new airway to Kennedy Airport, once again easily following its track by observing the batteries of high-altitude multi-barrelled anti-aircraft guns which line either side of the route. At Kennedy Airport, the disembarking passengers will be greeted by the welcoming combined choirs of the FBI and the CIA, and express processing of their papers and baggage will be carried out in our newly refurbished immigration lounge at Ellis Island.

(He sits down to somewhat muted applause and the Russian Air Minister rises to his feet. There is much clinking of glasses and cries of 'Za zdorovie')

RUSSIAN: *(Incisively)* Our plans for the arrival of the so-called reciprocal goodwill flight by an American wide-bodied jetliner from the deca- dent *(Corrects himself)* Democratic People's Republic of the United States of America are not so elaborate. In order to facilitate the crossing of the frontiers of our glorious Union of Soviet Socialist Republics we have established a new five-year airway plan. We have decreed that a clearly marked air-corridor which we have named the Igor Smutchnik Air-Corridor, after the great Russian scientist who discovered the Law of Gravity *(Glasses clink in toasts to this Slavic genius)* will commence at our extreme Western border – at the frontier town of Wrightskovsky, the birthplace of Wilburski and Orvilleovitch Wrightskovksy, the great Georgian pioneers of heavier-than-air flight. *(Again much clinking of vodka glasses is heard)*

From then on until the American jetliner lands at Moscow International Airport, there will be no elaborate so-called air-security arrangements – *provided* that the American jetliner keeps exactly to the Igor Smutchnik Air-Corridor. Should the navigation of the American airliner prove to be at fault, then *(He lowers his voice to a doom-laden whisper)* regrettably the aircraft will have entered Soviet restricted military air-space and will immediately be shot down, *(Hurriedly)* according to the terms of the unratified Helsinki Agree- ment, by our latest massed batteries of the new satellite-controlled Pippik missile. *(Murmurs of Russian assent)*

AMERICAN: *(Coldly)* How long is this new air-corridor?

RUSSIAN: One thousand two-hundred miles. Exactly.

AMERICAN: And how wide?

RUSSIAN: Two feet.

For some strange reason this sketch seems to have caught the imagination of listeners almost everywhere the English language is spoken. While this is very flattering to my insecure ego, I shall go to my grave wondering why it tickles the funny bone of so many people so consistently. It is, after all, only a five-minute recording of a man getting smashed out his mind.

THE TOAST MASTER

To a degree, 'The Toast Master' is based on fact. During my many years of cabaret, I have met and been 'introduced' by a large number of these imposing gentlemen. (Note: there are no Toast Mistresses – something that women's lib hasn't yet twigged.)

Of all the synthetic professions created for the luxury trade, the Toast Master's is probably the most dispensable. I'm not knocking these splendid men in their red 'tails', only the need for their august presence and services.

Personally I have always found them to be friendly and helpful, but I do know that to become one of their august body an applicant has to be 'one of them'. By this I mean that *influence* plays a large part in the selection which, incidentally, is otherwise totally unbiased. An applicant for the right to wear the Toast Master's get-up and carry the guild stamp of authority has got to be acceptable to the Hierarchy. It matters *who* you know.

He also has to be possessed of a rich, plummy voice that savours the introductions and toasts and he has to have a cheerful and weighty personality, to lend tone and authority to occasions which can range from Bar-Mitzvahs to golden weddings, from nuptials to jubilees.

The particular Toast Master upon whom I based this sketch has long since departed this vale of Toasts. He was a near dipsomaniac of great charm and (when sober) wit, and regularly got 'legless' during the course of the proceedings. This thumbnail sketch is a fondly-remembered tribute to his memory and to his efforts to get things right.

For those who might have known him, I will give you a clue – he was over six feet two inches tall and built like a brick outhouse. He was also Irish.

The top table of some terribly important political dinner in a Town Hall. Standing behind the chairman is the regal figure of the presiding Toast Master, glorious in his white tie and red tail-coat with his miniature medals tinkling gently over his breast pocket. His large, genial moon-face is brick-red, with more than a hint of high blood pressure besides the healthy tan of the outdoorsman. He is the picture of good fellowship. An ex-Irish guardsman, he has perfect elocution with no trace of his own ethnic accent in the plummy delivery of his professional speech.

On either side of the chairman are seated guests of great distinction and advanced age – of both sexes – most of them already well on the way to intoxication, having ploughed a wide furrow through champagne, sherry, burgundy, Sauternes and brandy. The loyal toast has already been given and thick cigar smoke is now wreathing the distinguished gathering in a poisonous cloud.

The Toast Master has, along with the guests, sampled each and every one of the wines and spirits, plus a fortifying amount of pink gin beforehand. This he consumed discreetly behind the curtains hiding the wine servery. He is holding his own, without any trace of inebriation, but he has yet to face a formidable barrage of toasts to come. He whispers in the chairman's ear, informing him of his intentions and gets a vague nod in assent. He straightens up and bangs his gavel down on the wooden block beside the chairman with a resounding clunk three times in quick succession.

TOAST MASTER: *(With great clarity)* My lords, ladies and gentlemen, His

Excellency the British Ambassador, Lord Fortescue, will take wine with His Excellency the Bessarabian Ambassador, Count Bobelescu.

(All rise a little unsteadily to their feet)

ALL: Count Bobelescu! *(They drink and then reseat themselves with an effort. During this time the Toast Master has also had a 'slurp' from a tray of drinks carried by a passing waiter)*

TOAST MASTER: *(Still without much uncertainty in his rich tones and once again banging down his gavel of office)* My lords, ladies and gentlemen, His Excellency the Bessarabian Ambassador, Count Bobelescu, will take wine with the British Ambassador, *(Pause)* Lord Fortescue. *(But he leaves out 'His Excellency' for the Brit)*

(All rise again and drink the toast – repeating it with slightly more effort)

ALL: Lord Fortescue! Good old George . . . . *(The last remark is muttered* sotto voce, *or rather* blotto voce*)*

TOAST MASTER: *(As soon as they are seated and having refreshed himself again from a passing tray of booze he aims his gavel a little uncertainly, thereby missing on the third clunk and hitting the tablecloth and a fork)* My lords, ladies and gentlemen, the British *(First slip)* Ambassadrels, *(He emphasizes her title with a beery smile in his voice)* Lady Forltescue, *(The liquor is having its effect)* will take wine with His Excellency the Bessarabian Ambassador, Count Bobelescu. *(The 'L's of the hard-drinking man are beginning to creep in)*

(Once again all rise, scraping back their chairs and by now the lords, ladies and gentlemen are getting smashed)

ALL: Count Bobalescu! First class fellah. For a wog. Bloody good show. Knockout. *(The words are slurred and somewhat out of synchronization)*

TOAST MASTER: *(Waiting till they have all, with 'ughs' and 'aahs' of effort, inaccurately attempted to reseat themselves)* My lords, ladies and gentlemal, *(The gavel has descended three times, registering one hit, one near miss and a brandy balloon glass)* His Excellelcy, Count *(Fiercely to get it right)* Bobalescuscu will take wile with the British Albassadress, *(Pause while he recollects the name)* Laly Foltescuel – Laly Foltescuel!

(All, who still can, rise with a great deal of effort to their table-supported feet and give the toast)

ALL: Laly Fortescuel! Laly Folescuel, good old Gertie! What a cracker. Gal in a milli . . .*(Hic)* milliol. Bloody lovely!

(Once more the guests thump down into their chairs, amid much hiccupping and the odd glass being knocked over. One chair falls over with a crash and a muttered 'Christ')

TOAST MASTER: *(Now well away and finding great difficulty with his gavel control)* My lols, *(Smashes a bottle)* lalies and . . . gent-men *(Hic)* geltmielmel. *(Another bottle goes)* The Briltish – Brilish Albassadol al the British Albalsad-drels. Lol an Laly Foltelscuel, will take wile . . . *(Sings 'Take wile')*. Ooh, they'll *take wile!* with the Bel – Belsarralbial Albal – Albalsadol, *(Memory eludes him)* Coult . . . Coult . . . *(He remembers)* Ah! Coult Bobala-bob . . . *(He giggles helplessly as he suddenly finds the name ridiculous but recovers with a colossal effort)* . . . Coult Bollaboll Abulescul! *(Terrific hiccup and the Toast Master passes clean out, collapsing with a disintegrating crash of silver, porcelain and glass into the centre spread of the top table)*

Note: This piece will always play better than it reads, for it is strictly a 'performer's' sketch, and the exact progression of getting plastered is very much a hit-and-miss affair. So is the gavel!

One thing that great television and radio networks cover with much skill and evident relish is civil disturbance, and they vie with each other to extract the most drama out of these sad proceedings.

This is a tribute to the on-the-spot reporters of our time.

THE PARIS RIOTS

A vista down a wide, deserted Paris street. Napoleon designed these picturesque avenues as the spokes of a wheel, emanating from his great Places. I know from experience that when tensions grow and the cry 'Aux Barricades' sounds anachronistically, the Garde Mobile or some other over-armed body of Gallic toughs appears as if by black magic, and the avenues empty of their fluid crowds as though a drain plug had been pulled. Bonaparte was an artillery expert and the great avenues are specifically designed for firing down with cannon. The French know this.

On to the scene comes the BBC commentator Roger Fudgeknuckle, his cable microphone clutched tightly in his tense right hand.

ROGER: *(Blaring into the mike)* One, two, three. *(Looks out of shot)* Oh! *(Immediately puts on his dramatic commentator's look of discerning bias)* This is Roger Fudgeknuckle. Reporting on the Paris Riots – dateline Paris. For the BBC. *(Nothing is happening and no one is in sight. Things have to be said, however, and Roger says them)* It's the calm before the storm. As well as the calm after last night's storm. There is a tremendous air of tension. The atmosphere is electric. *(A dog patters up and barks, then relieves itself against his leg)*

VOICE OFF: Get out of it. *(Something is thrown which hits the mutt. It limps off howling)*

ROGER: It only needs a spark to set Paris alight. So far there have been no actual fires, but the feeling is in the air – just one false move from the wrong people at the right moment and Paris will be burning. Don't be deceived by the apparent calm and the fact that no one appears to be on the streets. Behind every corner people could well be lurking. Even the cleverly concealed strategic outposts of the Garde Mobile are invisible to the naked eye. At first and . . . *(Pause)* . . . even second glance, this great avenue seems deserted but that is an illusion. Machinegun posts are probably everywhere.

(Sound of a truck moving to a grinding halt)

ROGER: This could be a mobile unit of the Garde Mobile. So-called, of course, because they are . . . *(Pause)* . . . mobile.

(Several voices off and heavy cables are dragged about. Enter Clyde Quigley of NBC, also equipped with a microphone)

CLYDE: *(Ignoring Roger)* And this is Clyde Quigley, your on-the-spot NBC news reporter, to bring you live satellite coverage of the disastrous Paris riots, which have set Paris aflame with revolutionary fervour. The cry is 'Aux Barricades'. To the barricades.

ROGER: *(Nettled, with his hand covering his mike)* I say, old man. This is my spot. I'm BBC. Roger Fudgeknuckle. Belt up, old chap, there's a good fellow.

CLYDE: *(Also covering his mike)* Button your lip, buster! This is *my* pitch. NBC always covers these Frog capers from here. It's our avenue, meathead. Move along.

ROGER: *(Furious)* What a bloody nerve. You rotten little guttersnipe. I'll complain to your Ambassador. You Yanks think you own the bloody world.

CLYDE: Jesus Christ, you colonial Imperialist faggot. That does it. Coming from you. You son-of-a-bitch. *(Shouts off)* Kowalski! Move his truck!

VOICE OFF: All right. All ready.

(Gears crunch and the NBC truck is deliberately driven into the BBC outside broadcast unit lorry)

BRITISH VOICE: *(Angrily)* What the bloody 'ell you fink you're doin' – you stupid Yankee git.

VOICE OFF: Harry! Clobber the Limey! *(Sound of heavy fisticuffs)*

SECOND YANK (VOICE OFF): Pull der door off his truck, Big Joe.

BIG JOE: OK, Louie.

(Door rips off and clangs down on the avenue cobbles)

BRITISH VOICE: I say! That's a bit strong. *(Heavy blows)* Bleedin' liberty.

ROGER: You asked for it. *(Thumps Clyde with his microphone, which is affected audibly, so is Clyde)*

CLYDE: Ouch! All right, Pilgrim. *(Heavy blow – plus ripping sound of tearing cloth – then a big punch obviously in the soft gut)*

ROGER: *(Gasps)* Ooh! My . . . ugh! You bastard! That was below the belt.

(Clyde and Roger wrestle on the ground, gouging and kicking with 'Oohs', 'Ughs' and 'Ouches'. The two truck crews charge each other's machines with appropriate yells of 'Smash his microwave antenna, Fred.' 'Kick his modulator in.' 'Rip out his squelch pack.' Much rending metal and shattering glass. A third truck pulls up with a squeal of brakes. Heavy clubbing is heard and cries of: 'Salaud!' 'Maquereaux!' 'Chameaux!' 'Pierrots.' 'Sod off! Sod off!' 'Mon Dieu! Les Russes.' 'Take your hands off me, frogspawn.' 'Go home, Tommy.' 'Yankee gangster. Fiche le camp!' Enter Pierre Crapaud, the Radio Diffusion Française commentator, excitedly commenting on the riot.)

PIERRE: Voici Pierre Crapaud pour les actualités de Radio Diffusion Française. Zut alors, mes amis. Quelle catastrophe! Juste à l'instant critique pendant les négociations entre les syndicats et le gouvernement, une autre explosion de violence! Excusez-moi. *(To Roger who is breathing hard while trying to strangle Clyde)* Êtes-vous socialiste? Communiste – ou Front Populaire? Vous, monsieur! Êtes-vous communiste?

CLYDE: *(Gasping)* Who the hell are you? Calling me a communist – you Frog. *(Hits Pierre. Roger hits as well)*

PIERRE: *(Teeth being spat out)* M'aidez! M'aidez! *(Joins the mêlée)* A moi!

(Rising vocal chorus of the 'Marseillaise'. Arrival of the Garde Mobile, etc.)

COMMENTATOR (MICHAEL BENTINE): Britain is famous throughout the world for its legends and myths, many of them based on historical fact. But the most famous 'invisible' exports in Britain are its ghosts – phantoms and hauntings. With me are Colonel Hector Plasm and Dr Luke Warm, who are acknowledged experts on the supernatural.

COLONEL: Para-normal.

MB: I beg your pardon, Colonel?

COLONEL: Para-normal as in para-chute, not super-normal as in super-kala fraga-listic expi-alli-docious.

MB: I see.

COLONEL: Ah, but you don't see. That's the whole *crux ansata* of the matter. Most ghosts are invisible. So you can't see them.

MB: Then you don't believe in ghosts?

COLONEL: Believe in them? Of course we believe in them. Otherwise we wouldn't hunt them.

MB: Hunt them?

COLONEL: Exactly. Dr Warm and I are ghost hunters. We track down the most dangerous invisible big game on earth – the ghosts of Great Britain.

DOCTOR: Aye, we do that. We go on safari after the ghosties and ghoulies and things that go bump in the night.

MB: Have you any concrete evidence?

COLONEL: No! Very few ghosts are made out of concrete. Most of our evidence is circumstantial, but we do have evidence.

DOCTOR: Such as our trophies. This is a photograph of the library at our headquarters at Howling Hall. As you can see, the walls are hung with our spoils of the chase.

COLONEL: Notice the trophy shields: each one the proud bearer of the big ghostly game that we have bagged.

MB: I can't see anything on the shields.

COLONEL: My dear sir, of course you can't. Wouldn't be a real ghost if you could. Now, look at that big shield, with the date 1966 on it, that one is the pride of our collection.

MB: But there's nothing there.

COLONEL: Precisely. Isn't it a beauty? How much did it weigh, doctor?

DOCTOR: Nothing.

> ## THE MOST HAUNTED HOUSE IN BRITAIN

COLONEL: *(Reverently)* A world record. By George, what a trophy! There for the whole world *not* to see is the living – I'm sorry – dead proof of what it's all about.

DOCTOR: It shakes the sceptics.

MB: Where did you get . . . ?

COLONEL: Bag. You don't *get* trophies, you bag them.

MB: All right, Colonel, where did you bag that one?

COLONEL: The usual place. The best ghost hunting ground there is – Grisly Grange, Grantham – where we made this historic recording of what is undoubtedly the most haunted house in Britain.

(Fade in tape effects: background of night sounds, owls hooting, insects in the grass, wind, etc.)

COLONEL: Dr Warm and I stationed ourselves just opposite the north wing, where the first of the nightly manifestations takes place.

MB: The first? You mean there is more than one ghost at Grisly Grange?

COLONEL: *(Short bark of a laugh)* More than one? There are crowds of them. Masses of monstrous manifestations. The whole Grange is packed with phantoms. Just look at *that* picture of it at midnight.

MB: Looks empty to me.

COLONEL: I told you. Packed from floor to ceiling – ghosts actually queue up to haunt it.

DOCTOR: Aye! The County Council are having to build an annexe to cope with the overflow.

MB: I don't believe it. You're having me on.

COLONEL: Never more serious in all my present reincarnation. In fact, dead serious.

(Sound of hollow groan and echoing footsteps on stone; exterior perspective)

MB: What's that?

COLONEL: That is the ghost of the First Earl – he goes third. I'm sorry. I mean the Third Earl – he goes first. *(Voice level drops)* There he walks along the high battlements; the top turret door opens *(It does so)* and the gaunt ghostly figure in shining armour enters the attic of the great turret . . .

(Hollow groan, then sound of a ghost in full armour falling down a spiral flight of stone stairs. It finishes with a final metallic crunch and a 'badly hurt' groan)

COLONEL: We must get that top step replaced.

MB: Is that all?

COLONEL: Great Vincent Price, no! After midnight comes the second ghost, the moaning monk. He walks the groaning gallery from ten minutes past midnight till half-past midnight. Then it's the turn of the nattering nun. She natters from half-past twelve till one o'clock – British occult double summer time.

(Sound of moaning monk moaning away, as his ghostly sandals slap along an echoing gallery floor)

MOANING MONK: Oh, unhappy monk am I! Oh, woe is me! Mea culpa! Mea culpa! What a monastic turn-up for the Doomsday Book! Oh, unhappy Benzedrictine Brother that I am – sleepless for eternity.

(A female ghostly echoing voice breaks in, approaching – small shoes slapping along the same corridor)

FEMALE GHOST: *(Speaking very fast)* Oh no! I said, Reverend Mother, Sister Mercy has got it all wrong. It was not Sister Hysteria who was found in the summer house with the under-gardener by Father O'Reilly, but rather Father O'Reilly who was caught with Sister Hysteria in the summer house by the under-gardener, Reverend Mother.

COLONEL: Oh dear! That is the nattering nun. She's early. No sense of time – female phantoms.

MOANING MONK: Oh dear, oh dear, oh dear! What a calamity! You're too soon. You're not appearing here till after half-past twelve. Go away.

NATTERING NUN: Don't tell me when to haunt and when *not* to haunt, you male chauvinist monastic pig, you.

MOANING MONK: The Father Abbot made it quite clear to your Reverend Mother – no nattering nuns till after the monks have finished moaning.

NATTERING NUN: Moan, moan, moan, you're never satisfied, you miserable monk. Take, take, take. All you think about is yourself. You're all self-centred, egotistical, selfish – never a thought for others. No wonder you're earthbound. Demonic! That's what you are – diabolic, unfeeling, unethical, typical male.

MOANING MONK: *(Trying to get a moan in edgewise)* Now, now, Sister!

NATTERING NUN: Take your filthy skeletal hands off my habit! I know you Benzedrictines. You're always so *holy* on the outside and rotten to the core on the inside. You cloistered sex-maniac, you. Take that!

(Heavy blows from her rosary on the invisible Brother's skeletal frame, followed by the sound of scattered beads)

NATTERING NUN: Now, look what you've done! You've broken my bloody rosary.

(Tape cuts off)

COLONEL: She's always the same on double summer time. She forgets to adjust her hour glass. Now here's a fascinating manifestation.

(Sound of light female footsteps on gravel. Door opens. Weeping ghostly girl's voice is heard as she ascends the echoing wooden staircase to the second floor. Window opens with a creak and she flings herself out to land on the gravel – broken neck sound – picks herself up and repeats the action, a little faster each time)

GIRL'S VOICE: Oh! I have been wronged. I have been wronged. Oh, I have been wronged. Oh, *how* I have been wronged. Oh, how *wronged* I have been. Ooh! I *have*. Wronged. *Wronged.* Ooh! I have! Been wronged! *(Her speed increases the whole time)*

COLONEL: *(Voice over)* That's the wronged chambermaid. She was wronged by the wicked Lord Bashing. She never got over it. Chucked herself out of the window on to the gravel below. Tragic!

(The wronged chambermaid is now re-enacting her 'up-tempo' suicide at treble speed – and getting faster)

COLONEL: Oh dear! She does go on so. I can't stand wingeing women.

MB: How tragic! The wicked Lord Bashing must have wronged her terribly.

DOCTOR: No! She went potty when he *stopped*. Couldn't live without her nightly wronging. Bad show!

(Sound of galloping hooves and rattling wheels as a fast-driven phantom coach thunders round the drive)

MB: What's that?

DOCTOR: The Headless Coachman – always appears about now – driving the phantom coach with the ghost of Lady Codswallop inside. The fiery steeds pull the racing coach at breakneck speed down the long drive while *he* sits up on the box, the reins in his headless hands.

(The coach goes full-tilt into the trees)

COLONEL: Happens every night, poor blighter. Can't see a thing.

(Sound of revolving wheels of upturned coach. Inside its ectoplasmic wreck Lady Codswallop yells ghostly abuse)

LADY CODSWALLOP: You great clumsy oaf! Why can't you look where you're going? You've broken my bloody neck again. You're fired, you moron. I'll have your ghostly guts for garters. Don't just stand there. Put your head on and help me out. Berk!

(Sounds of weird wet slobbering as a great thing climbs out of the weed-covered moat)

COLONEL: Listen to that! Sets your teeth on edge, eh? Raises the hairs at the back of the neck, eh?
MB: What on earth?
DOCTOR: Very little to do with earth. It's an extra-dimensional Denizen of the Pit. A monstrous demon of the abyss.
COLONEL: The great fire monster of Grisly Grange, *(Pause)* Grantham.

(Crackling flames and hissing sounds as the great fire-bug ponderously makes its way towards the house, its huge plodding feet sucking out of the mud and slapping down on to the crunching gravel. It roars like a dinosaur as it proceeds. Terrified screams from the ghosts inside the Grange. Ghostly voice montage)

NATTERING NUN: Oh, Holy Reverend Mother! It's the fire monster. Oh, saints preserve us. Quick, Sister Melancholia. Ring the bell! Ring the bell!

(Bell starts ringing)

MOANING MONK: Oh, woe is me! No peace for the wicked. A monk can't even moan in peace nowadays. Blasted flaming monstrosity.
THIRD EARL: *(Muffled in clanking bent armour)* All hands to the pump! Get that bucket-chain going!
WRONGED CHAMBERMAID: Oh, I have been wronged. Oh you fire monster, you. I have been wronged. What about a hot quickie?
FIRE MONSTER: *(Roaring and crackling)* Aaargh! *(Sounds of fire-engine arriving – ghostly instructions)*
VOICES: Get that fire out in the east wing! Get the hoses going! *(Hoses start)* More buckets of water! *(Buckets thrown and hissing steam, monster yells of fiery rage and hissing)*
MB: Good Lord! a ghostly fire brigade.
COLONEL: Naturally. Happens every night. Otherwise the Grange would have been burned down years ago.

(Tape fades on effects)

MB: How did you get started as ghost hunters? I mean, what qualifications do you need to become one?

COLONEL: *(Chuckling)* You need to understand the workings of the ghostly mind.

DOCTOR: *(Giggling)* Aye! Sort of . . . set a thief to catch a thief. *(His laugh becomes ghostly and fades away as they both vanish with appropriate ghostly ironic laughter)*

COLONEL: *(Fading on echo)* See you at Grisly Grange . . .

DOCTOR: *(Also fading)* Grantham.

(Their maniacal laughter dissolves into thin echoing air)

THE NATO GENERALS

It has always struck me as odd that military men work out their strategy with war-games or, as the Wehrmacht called them, *Kriegspielen*, although it is a fact that General Marck, a one-legged Wehrmacht Corps Commander in the Second World War and a fanatical war-gamer, worked out that the Allied invasion forces would strike on the Normandy beaches and not in the Pas de Calais area, which all of the top German brass believed to be the plan.

The popularity of war-games at a commercial level and the widespread enjoyment of the 'Dungeons and Dragons' type of table games has grown exponentially, which is probably due to the long period of peace since the Second World War.

I wrote this sketch in the fifties. It expresses my concern that manoeuvres on a sand-table with little model tanks and guns could affect the lives of millions of people. Long may it all remain a game!

(Oddly enough this sketch works as well on radio – in pure sound – as on television and the stage. I have played it on all three media in the US, Australia and the UK.)

(Impressive doom-laden voice over dramatic music)

VOICE: Here at NATO headquarters, high-ranking military commanders are busily working out the master plan for the defence of the NATO alliance. Generals from the United States of America, Great Britain, West Germany and Turkey are involved in a simulated attack and defence exercise of Western democracy.

(Around the large contoured sand-table are the four generals. The table-top is neatly divided into battle zones, labelled appropriately with the name of each country's sector. The British General is a dapper and rather aggressively cheerful character whose flattened 'Rs' remind one of Field Marshal Montgomery's. Beside him on the right is the German General (a large, stockily built Bundeswehr commander, complete with duelling scars and monocle) and on the left the US commander, while the Turkish General is standing at the other side of the table.)

BRITISH GENERAL: Well now, gentlemen, I think our plan 'B' would be best in these circumstances. We will attack on this narrow front here, utilizing 500 of our new Mark Five battle tanks.

(As he says this the General moves a tank with his swagger-cane, and addresses the last part of his speech to the German General)

GERMAN GENERAL: Was ist los, Herr General? *(Obviously he hasn't caught the British General's drift)*

BRITISH GENERAL: The Mark Five. We will carry out the manoeuvres using Mark Five tanks. *(He speaks more deliberately and louder)* Mark Fünf!

(The German commander still looks puzzled)

BRITISH GENERAL: Oh, blast it! Where's the interpreter? *(He calls off)* Colonel Witherspoon! Can you come over here a minute?

(A smart, grey-haired and very cool British Colonel marches over and whacks up a sizzling salute)

WITHERSPOON: Sir! *(He pronounces it 'Sah'!)*

BRITISH GENERAL: Witherspoon, will you tell General von Spitzen-Schnauzer that we're carrying out the manoeuvre using the Mark Five tank.

WITHERSPOON: Sah! *(He moves two steps over to the German General and stamps his feet as he salutes)* Herr General von Spitzen-Schnauzer.

GENERAL SPITZEN-SCHNAUZER: Herr Oberst. *(He clicks his heels)*

WITHERSPOON: Wir haben ein manoeuvre ausführen der Panzer Nummer Fünf. Verstehen Sie, mein General?

GENERAL SPITZEN-SCHNAUZER: Bestimmt, Herr Oberst. *(He nods his head vigorously)* Jawohl. Sehr gut.

WITHERSPOON: *(Saluting and stamping feet again)* Sah! *(He returns and salutes the British General, who acknowledges him with a casual wave of his swagger-cane)*

BRITISH GENERAL: First class, Witherspoon. Tell General Ahmed Ben Dova, the Turkish chap, will you!

WITHERSPOON: *(With another salute and stamp)* Sah! *(He marches round the table and starts to translate the information)*

WITHERSPOON: *(After yet another salute and foot stamping)* General Ben Dova, salaam aleikum!

TURKISH GENERAL: Aleikum es salaam!

(The British interpreter now goes into a 'crud' Arabic-cum-Turkish translation, carefully followed by the little Turkish General, a fiery-looking bearded Moslem)

WITHERSPOON: Al bar mak melea mal me bara baleah muk-muk, mea lac bara ach mala Mark Five moolu al ballah!

(His hands meanwhile graphically emphasize the main points of the instructions in a dramatic and most unBritish fashion. The little Turk repeats the odd word during this short speech and makes similar gestures)

WITHERSPOON: *(Salutes and stamps his feet yet again)* Dal mah habla dea! Allah illay Akbar!

(The Turkish General and Witherspoon exchange the touching the forehead, lips, etc., ritual greeting. Witherspoon now marches back to the British General and whacks up another salute)

BRITISH GENERAL: Well done, Witherspoon. Oh dear, I nearly forgot General Knockenlocker, the American commander.

(Witherspoon salutes the British General, then swings round and strolls – he does

not *march – over to the American General, who is playing with a model tank. Witherspoon adopts an American accent and plays the scene like Marlon Brando)*

WITHERSPOON: *(Now relaxed and sighing and breathing through his nose, his thumbs in his belt)* General Knockenlocker, sir! *(He gives the American salute)*

(The American General acknowledges lazily)

GENERAL KNOCKENLOCKER: Colonel? What can I do for you, Mac? *(He obviously hasn't understood the British General's instructions)*

WITHERSPOON: Permission to speak, General?

GENERAL KNOCKENLOCKER: Sure, why not? OK!

WITHERSPOON: Well, it's like this, General. We're gonna carry out de goddamn manoeuvres using der stinkin' Mark Five tank. Ya get me? *(Witherspoon digs the General in the ribs with his swagger-cane)*

GENERAL KNOCKENLOCKER: I gotcha.

WITHERSPOON: Great. *(He spins round and smartly salutes the British General)* All understood, sah!

BRITISH GENERAL: Splendid, Witherspoon. Don't know what I'd do without you. Now, what about a nice cup of tea? *(He beams round at the other generals)* Eh what? *(He bangs down his swagger-cane on the sand-table and smashes the German General's tank)*

GENERAL SPITZEN-SCHNAUZER: *(Instantly reacting in fury)* Was machen Sie, Herr General? Mein Panzer! *(He tenderly picks up the smashed model tank and examines it)* Dummkopf. Mein Panzer ist kaputt! *(He is already in tears)*

BRITISH GENERAL: *(To Witherspoon)* What is he talking about? I never touched his bloody panzy. Tell him, Witherspoon!

(Witherspoon marches over to the German General and stamp-salutes. The German is furious)

WITHERSPOON: Herr General?

GENERAL SPITZEN-SCHNAUZER: Verdammt noch einmal, Herr Oberst! General Smythe-Smythe hat meinen lieben Panzer, meinen kleinen Panzer kaputt gemacht!

GENERAL SMYTHE-SMYTHE: I say, I think I understood that. I never went near the bloody thing.

(Before Witherspoon can reply, the Turkish General indicates that he saw him do it)

TURKISH GENERAL: *(Pointing at his eye)* Al bea maha bechar malda maha bea muk-muk. Al ill al ballah! Bloody tank!

GENERAL SMYTHE-SMYTHE: Witherspoon, tell him to keep his bloody great nose out of it.

WITHERSPOON: *(Losing his cool a bit)* Bloody great nose, sir, out of it. Certainly, sir! *(He hurries over and stamp-salutes)*

WITHERSPOON: Allah mahakbar Smythe-Smythe beleyha malaba – snozzola – baham imshi!

(The Turkish General goes bananas – calling on the Gods to witness his being so insulted. He draws his sword and clouts the American General's tank by mistake. The laid-back General Knockenlocker suddenly reacts in fury)

GENERAL KNOCKENLOCKER: Colonel Witherspoon! At the double!

(Witherspoon turns round, ending with a smart double speed stamp salute)

WITHERSPOON: Sah!

GENERAL KNOCKENLOCKER: *(Shaking with barely suppressed rage)* You tell that no-good son of a Bedouyne Ayrab to keep his cotton-pickin', chicken-pluckin' hands offen ma tyank. *(The General has become very Texan)* D'ya hear?

WITHERSPOON: Yes, sir! *(Salutes)* Very good, sir. Cotton-picking.

(The British General interrupts him)

GENERAL SMYTHE-SMYTHE: *(Very deliberately)* Chicken-plucking! And do be most frightfully careful.

WITHERSPOON: *(Salutes, doubles over to the heavily breathing Turk and salutes with his usual stamp, hitting his shin painfully)* Oh sh . . . General Ben Dova, achma bala Ben Ben Bili maha ach daba debra ma *(He searches for the word cotton-pickin')* cotton maha picky-picky. Millah mahala Ben. *(He gives up on chicken-pluckin' and semi-mimes it)* Cluck, cluck, cluck, cluck, aagh!

GENERAL BEN DOVA: *(Beside himself)* Cluck, cluck, cluck! Smythe-Smythe Allah ma billah. Mafeesh! Mafeesh! Mastouf!

GENERAL SMYTHE-SMYTHE: Witherspoon! What did he call me? What did he say?

WITHERSPOON: *(Desperately trying to ameliorate the explosive situation)* Well, sir, loosely translated, it means that he suggests that you go and visit the House of Abdul the Taxidermist.

GENERAL SMYTHE-SMYTHE: *(Goes ape)* I'll teach that sawn-off little camel jockey to tell me to get stuffed! Take that! *(Down comes the swagger-cane on the Turkish tank)*

(The Turk explodes. He again smashes the American tank)

GENERAL KNOCKENLOCKER: Okay, ya no good desert Gofer. This means war. You just smashed ma tyank.

(The Generals start firing their little artillery pieces which are decorating the table, issuing imaginary orders to different units)

GENERAL SMYTHE-SMYTHE: All units advance to position 'Y'. Stand by to scramble the 'Tornadoes', Witherspoon. Bang! Bang! Bang! Bang!

GENERAL SPITZEN-SCHNAUZER: Achtung! Achtung! Panzergrenadiere vorwärts! Macht schnell! Sturzkampfgeschwader im Angriff!

(General Ben Dova is shrieking Turkish orders and oaths in all directions interspersed with the Turkish equivalent of Bang! Bang! noises)

GENERAL KNOCKENLOCKER: That does it. I'm going nuclear. I'm pressing the Tit.

(A mini-rumbling commences and the rushing sound of steam heralds the take-off effects of a small model rocket which climbs majestically up into the ceiling of the war-game room – through which it punches a hole – continuing upwards until out of earshot. There is a stunned silence, broken by the British General)

GENERAL SMYTHE-SMYTHE: Well, that about does it. Now, by my calculations, we've all got about four minutes left. Who's for a cup of instant tea?

I wrote this sketch twenty-three years ago. It is now oddly prophetic.

ARMED POLICE

ANNOUNCER: It has never been the policy of the British police constabularies to allow the bobby on the beat to carry firearms. The British copper is expected to keep the peace without the use of gunfire – only drawing and using his truncheon to defend himself against physical attack, or to subdue a criminal who is endangering the public. From time to time, of course, specialist police marksmen have had to be called in. This is the inevitable response to the growing threat of international terrorism. However, the ordinary police forces would find themselves in some difficulties if arms were issued indiscriminately for everyday use.

(Street perspective: a London Square. Pigeons and distant traffic. Heavy-booted feet move purposefully into presence. A police car with siren pulls up and the car doors open.)

INSPECTOR: Right men! Now, *no* shooting unless it's absolutely necessary. You have been issued with a revolver and six rounds of ammunition; only shoot when I give the order. Give me the loud-hailer, Sergeant.

SERGEANT: Very good, sir.

INSPECTOR: *(Into Tannoy)* Testing: one, two, three. Right. *(Loudly on filter effect)* Come on out. We know you're in there. Just come out quietly with your hands up.

(Window breaks)

VOICE: *(Shouting)* Never, copper. Come in and get me. *(Shots fired with ricochets)*

INSPECTOR: Take cover, men. Sergeant, cover me with two shots through that window.

SERGEANT: Right, sir. *(Fires two shots. Glass breaks)*

VOICE INSIDE: Take that, you pigs. *(Shots are fired and ricocheting bullets spang off the pavement)*

(Milk-cart pulls up)

MILKMAN: 'Ere, I've got to deliver the milk to Number Eleven.

INSPECTOR: Oh, well, all right, we'll cover you. Make it snappy. Two shots each, men. *(Shots from bluebottles as the milkman scurries up to the door and rings the bell)*

MILKMAN: Milk – O!

(Door opens – two shots from house)

VOICE: Oh! Two pints, please. Got any cream? *(Fires)*

MILKMAN: I'll drop some in on the way back. That will be two pounds for this week.

VOICE: Oh, right! *(Coins clink as the money changes hands)*

(Milkman scurries off and electric milk-cart drives away)

VOICE: Come and get me, coppers. *(More shots from house)*

INSPECTOR: Right, Sergeant. Give him one round of tear gas.

SERGEANT: Sir! Smithers, tear gas.

(A dull report is heard and a crash of glass as the smoke-bomb goes through the window. A hissing sound is heard from inside the house and the man is soon coughing and spluttering. The shooting stops)

VOICE: All right. You win, copper. I'm coming out.

INSPECTOR: Come out with your hands up, but throw your gun out first!

VOICE: *(Coughing)* OK. *(Gun thrown out on to pavement)*

INSPECTOR: Cover him, men! Sergeant, put the cuffs on him. *(Footsteps quickly across the pavement)*

VOICE: *(Coughing)* I'll come quietly. *(Handcuffs are put on)*

INSPECTOR: Well done, men. Now bring Slasher Johnson to the station. I must caution you, Johnson, that anything you say will be taken down and may be used in evidence against you.

VOICE OF CRIMINAL: 'Ere! My name's not Slasher Johnson. I'm Basher Brownlow.

INSPECTOR: But isn't this Number Eleven, Pilkington Square?

BROWNLOW: No, mate. This is Number Eleven, Pilkington *Crescent*.

INSPECTOR: I'm sorry, Mr Brownlow. It's our mistake. Take the cuffs off him, Sergeant. *(Cuffs are removed)*

BROWNLOW: Oh, that's all right. Happens all the time.

INSPECTOR: Good day! Right, men. Pilkington Square.

(The booted feet march off round the corner, while the police car doors close and it roars off, its siren beeping)

*S*ound perspective of an open-air crowd at an airfield. There is the noise of jets and propeller-driven aircraft, and the gasps of the wondering throng convey all the excitement of a great air display. A commentator (à la Ray Baxter) is enthusiastically chattering away.

THE AIR DISPLAY

COMMENTATOR: And this is Arthur Spruill reporting from Farnborough Air Show. Once again this great International Air Display is dominated by the genius of British air technology. The new Wombat aircraft, with which the Royal Air Force will be equipped by 1998 is a masterpiece of advanced engineering. The airframe of this revolutionary aeroplane is made in Germany; the side-by-side twin-jet engines are French; the avionics, which virtually fly the aircraft from take-off to touch-down, are American; the new fully-castoring undercarriage is Italian and, of course, the ashtray is British. So is the pilot, Squadron Leader Bill Crackling of 700 Squadron. And here he comes making a low pass at zero feet right across the airfield – over the greenhouses of the Royal Horticultural Society. *(Roar of jet and endless breaking glass, as the Wombat's slipstream takes most of the panes of glass out of the nursery)* What a wonderfully cool display of sheer low-flying skill and total lack of consideration. And what a day it has been! We've seen the Royal Navy's new anti-submarine search-and-find aircraft, the Mark Five Wright Bi-plane, and the Army's latest short-range ground-to-air 'catapult', made entirely here in Britain from Malaysian rubber. And now comes the highlight of the show, the close- formation exhibition of superb airmanship by the Red Bears, Soviet Russia's brilliant visiting team of ace fighter-pilots, the pride of the Soviet Air Force, flying their new long-range Yakovlev 'Samovars', that revolutionary new Russian fighter that so closely resembles the latest revolutionary new American fighter, the Bald Eagle. And here they come. *(Sound of low-level diving 'pass' low over the airfield)*

TANNOY VOICE: *(On wobbly echo)* And that was the thrilling arrival of the Red Bears all the way from Soviet Russia. *(Very thin applause from the Soviet Embassy team)*

SPRUILL: That tremendous welcome came from the awe-struck crowd, literally speechless with admiration at the spectacle of this mass formation of Russian ground-attack fighters, armed with their latest 'Dosvidanya' missiles – the so-called 'goodbye' weapons, which were developed in Soviet Russia by a brilliant team of British defectors. *(Sound of jet formation circling the airfield in the distance)* This display by the Red Bears will be the highlight of the air display, in contrast to the earlier close-formation exhibition given by the Royal Air Force's new three-plane high altitude display team, which would undoubtedly have had an equal impact on the British public had it been visible to the naked eye.

TANNOY: During the display by the Red Bears all the instructions by the formation leader, Major Vladimir Nijinsky, will be heard as he leads his highly-trained formation through a veritable ballet of the air.

SPRUILL: Yes! These Commies – er – Russian pilots have really got their act together. An impressive blend of flying skill and discipline and sheer courage – each pilot carefully selected for his superb airmanship and his personal unlikelihood of asking for political asylum. And here they come. *(A low rumbling roar)* And the Red Bears do a low-pass over the remaining green houses of the Royal Horticultural Society. *(Breaking of more glass)* And straight up they go in a spectacular climbing chandelle.

(Russian-accented voice over the Tannoy, with jet noise in the background)

LEADER: Formation leader to Red Bears; close up number two. Three and four ready to break. Five and six drop back. Seven, eight and nine prepare to change to sickle formation, and ten . . . *(Pause)*

TEN: Da?

LEADER: Prepare to eject. You're on fire!

TEN: Da, da. *(Ejects)*

SPRUILL: And what a superb sight they make. The ten – no – nine Samovars tightly bunched together, with one of them diving vertically to the ground while the pilot swings safely below in his gaily-coloured parachute – a most unusual manoeuvre. *(Applause from the crowd)* Oh, and there goes the tenth Samovar into the Royal Horticultural Society's last greenhouse. *(Crash of glass and a very distant voice: 'You bastards!')*

RUSSIAN LEADER: *(Over Tannoy)* Close up three and four. Five take ten's position. Six and seven prepare to pass across formation. *(Crackle)*

(Telephone rings)

INTERRUPTING VOICE: Hello! Is that Farnborough 3925? Could I speak
to Gladys, please?

LEADER: Gladys? *(Pronounces it Glad-yis)*

VOICE: Yes, Gladys. This is Fred.

LEADER: *(Plus crackle of conversation of other pilots in formation)* Gladys?
Fred? Who is Fred? Are you Fred, number two?

TWO: No, I'm Ivan.

THREE: No, *I'm* Ivan.

FOUR: *I'm* Ivan.

FIVE: No, *I'm* Ivan.

SIX: You can't be. *I'm* Ivan.

SEVEN: *I'm* Ivan.

LEADER: Are you Ivan, Ivan?

FRED: No, I'm Fred. Can I speak to Gladys, please?

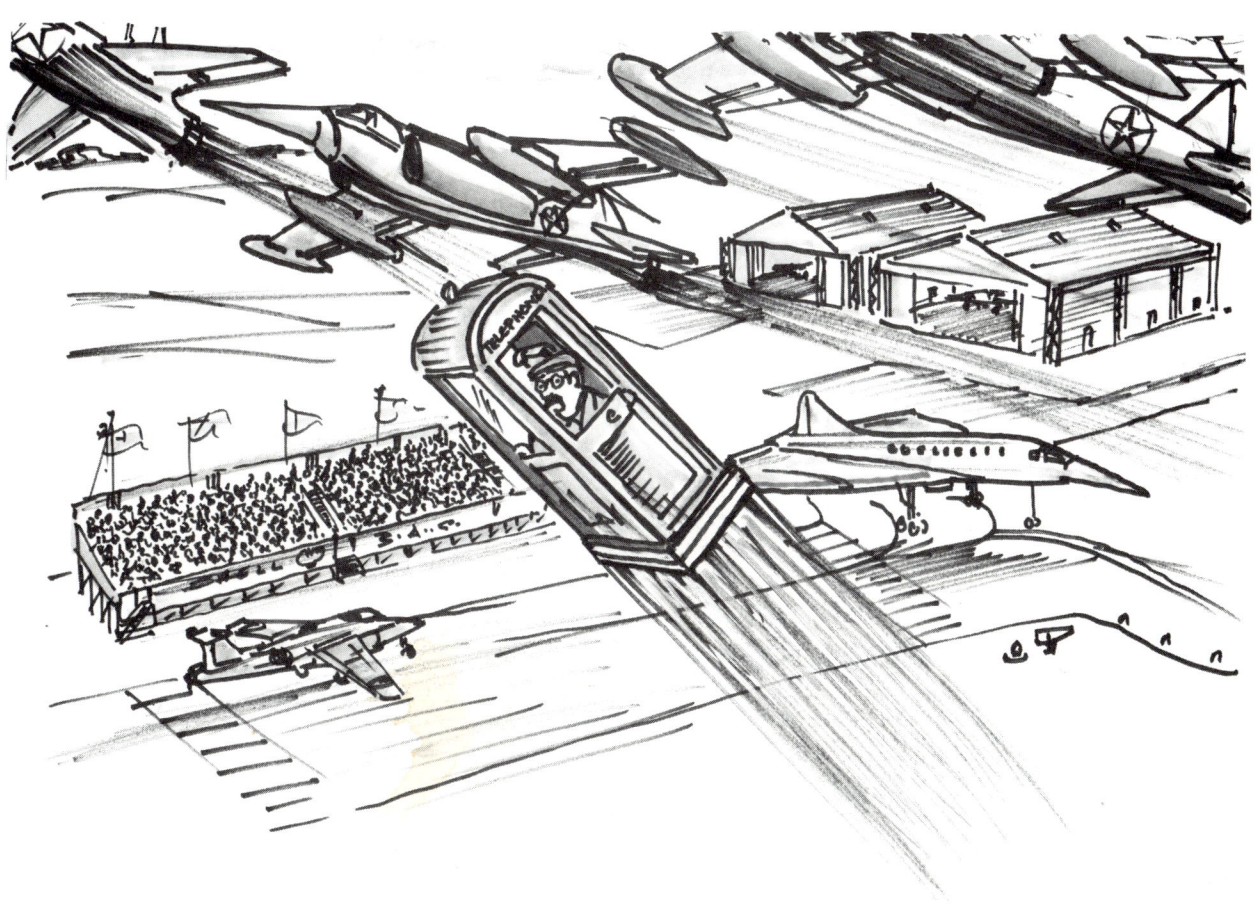

PILOTS: Ah, Gladys. Oh, Gladys. Sure, Gladys. Good old Gladys. Gladys. Hey comrades, it's Gladys. Gladys.

LEADER: Where are you, Fred?

FRED: I'm in a telephone box outside the station. Where are you?

LEADER: I'm at thirty-two thousand feet over Farnborough. You're too low, Fred. Climb immediately and join the formation.

FRED: Oh . . . *(Pause)* Right. *(Sound of coin button being pressed. Coins drop into box and telephone box takes off – to climb up to join the Red Bears)*

LEADER: Take number ten's position, Fred. All other aircraft close up.

VOICE: Da, da, da, da, da, da! Roger!

LEADER: Prepare to execute final manoeuvre. Prince of Wales Feathers. *(Slight pause)* Correction: Russian Eagle's Feathers. Execute!

(Sound of Samovars and Fred executing manoeuvre to terrific crowd cheers)

SPRUILL: What a magnificent sight they make – the nine gleaming Samovars and the Farnborough telephone box in perfect formation, as they come thundering down over the airfield to give their final salute, by firing their 'Dosvidanya' missiles into the grounds of the Royal Horticultural Society.

(They do so)

Among the annals of violent crimes in Britain the siege of Sydney Street stood alone, until the siege of the Iranian Embassy eclipsed it.

Before the First World War Anarchists, as they were then called, had holed themselves up in a house in the East End of London. Winston Churchill, who was Home Secretary at the time, took personal, on-the-spot charge of the large numbers of armed police and guardsmen who stormed the building. There was, of course, nothing funny about the deaths of several policemen, murdered in cold blood, or the deaths of the Anarchists themselves.

This piece emerged from the idea of taking the siege of Sydney Street and treating it like an episode of a television soap opera, such as *Coronation Street*.

SYDNEY STREET

MB: The long-running *Coronation Street* on ITV has prompted the BBC to challenge it with a similar series of their own.

We proudly present *Sydney Street*, based on the simple, everyday lives of an East End Jewish community before the First World War.

The interior of a small Victorian 'two up-two down' terraced house in London. Clinking of teacups and plates being washed up in an enamelled sink. Cutlery being laid heavily down on a table. Woman humming to herself. Rocking chair.

(Knock at door. It opens. Enter booted man)

MAN: 'Allo, Rose. 'Allo, Maurice.
MAURICE: 'Allo, Sam.
ROSE: *(At sink)* 'Allo, Sam.
MAURICE: Like a cup – lemon tea, Sam?
SAM: Ta! I'd like that, Maurice.
MAURICE: Rose, fetch Sam a cup of tea! Sit, Sam! Enjoy!
SAM: So? What's new?
MAURICE: The sink's blocked again.
ROSE: Yes. The sink's blocked again, Sam.

(Pause)

SAM: Oh! Probably the tea leaves. *(Takes the tea and slurps it)*
MAURICE: Take a biscuit, Sam! Enjoy!
SAM: Ta! *(Crunches biscuit)* A *good* biscuit, Rose.
ROSE: I make good biscuits.
MAURICE: Rose makes a good biscuit, Sam.

(Knock on door)

MAURICE: Come!

(Door opens. Enter another man)

MAN: 'Allo, Maurice.
MAURICE: 'Allo, Sid.
SID: 'Allo, Rose.
ROSE: 'Allo, Sid.
SID: 'Allo, Sam.
SAM: 'Allo, Sid.
ROSE: You like a cup – lemon tea, Sid?
SID: Thank you, Rose.
MAURICE: 'Ave a biscuit.
SID: Ta!
SAM: They're good biscuits. I've 'ad two.
ROSE: You've 'ad three – but who's counting?
MAURICE: Sit, Sid! Enjoy!
SID: Ta! *(Chair effects)* So what's new, Maurice?
MAURICE: The sink's blocked again.
ROSE: Yes, the sink's blocked, Sid.
SID: Probably the tea leaves.
SAM: I *told* Maurice that. I said: 'Probably the tea leaves.'
ROSE: Yes, Sam said that. I heard him. Sam said that.
MAURICE: Rose is right. That's what Sam said.
SAM: Yes. I said: 'Probably the tea leaves.' *(Pause while they all munch)*

(Knock on door)

MAURICE: Come!

(Door opens. Boots in)

MAN: 'Allo, Maurice.
MAURICE: 'Allo, Izzy.
IZZY: 'Allo, Rose.
ROSE: 'Allo, Izzy.

IZZY: 'Allo, Sam.

SAM: 'Allo, Izzy.

IZZY: 'Allo, Sid.

SID: 'Allo, Izzy.

MAURICE: Sit, Izzy! have a cup – lemon tea.

IZZY: Ta, Moishe. *(Tea effects)*

ROSE: 'Ave a biscuit, Izzy. I make a good biscuit. *(Munching from all three men)*

IZZY: You do, Rose. You do. A *nice* biscuit.

SID: 'Sa good biscuit. *(Munches)*

SAM: A *fine* biscuit . . . *(Munches and sips tea)* Rose makes!

MAURICE: Rose makes a good biscuit, Rose does.

IZZY: So. What's new, Moishe?

MAURICE: The sink's blocked again.

IZZY: Probably the tea leaves.

MAURICE: Sam said that, too.

SAM: Yes, I said: 'The tea leaves. It's probably the tea leaves.' So did Sid. Didn't you, Sid?

SID: Yes, I did. I said: 'Probably the tea leaves.' Like Sam I said.

ROSE: That's what's done it. The tea leaves.

(During this exchange the siege has started and runs parallel with the family dialogue)

POLICE: We know you're in there. Come on out! It's the police.

(Glass breaks)

FOREIGNER: Nevair! You filthy Capitalist running dogs! *(Shots from Mauser 9 M/M automatic pistol. Groans)*

POLICE: Take cover! Get the back-up reinforcements!

VOICE: Right, Sergeant. *(Running feet up street)*

(More shots)

POLICE: If you don't come out we're coming in to get you. We've sent for armed reinforcements. Throw down your guns!

SECOND FOREIGNER: Long live the Revolution! *(More shots and ricochets, groans, etc. More police arrive)*

POLICE: Right, men. Take cover in the doorways! The guards are coming.

(Military marching feet)

103

VOICE: Halt! Take cover! Fire when I give the order! Sergeant!

SERGEANT: Sah! *(Salute – feet stamping on cobbles)*

VOICE: Take four men and set up the Maxim gun in one of these houses – that one over there!

SERGEANT: Very good, sir. Johnson, Smith, MacTavish, Jones, follow me! We'll set up the gun in this house here. Break the door in!

(Door smashed in. Many more shots from guardsmen with rifles and from the besieged Anarchists. Glass shatters. Ricochets. Meanwhile, inside the house: knock on door)

MAURICE: Come!

(Door opens. More booted footsteps)

MAN: 'Allo, Maurice.

MAURICE: 'Allo, Rabbi.

RABBI: 'Allo, Rose.

ROSE: 'Allo, Rabbi.

RABBI: 'Allo, Sam.

SAM: 'Allo, Rabbi.

RABBI: 'Allo, Sid.

SID: 'Allo, Rabbi.

RABBI: 'Allo, Izzy. So what's new?

IZZY: 'Allo, Rabbi. Moishe says the sink's blocked again.

RABBI: Probably the tea leaves.

SAM: I said so. 'Probably the tea leaves.'

IZZY: Yes, Sam said so, so did Sid.

MAURICE: Yes, Sid did. Didn't you, Sid?

SID: Yes, I did. I said: 'Probably the tea leaves.'

IZZY: So did I, Rabbi. When Moishe said the sink was blocked again, I said:'Probably the tea leaves.'

ROSE: Cup lemon tea, Rabbi?

RABBI: Tenk you, Rose. Perhaps a biscuit?

MAURICE: Help yourself, Rabbi. Enjoy! Rose makes a fine biscuit.

SAM: A fine biscuit, Rabbi.

SID: Rose's biscuits are good, Rabbi.

SAM: Such a biscuit, Rose makes, Rabbi.

IZZY: The best. I always say, Rose makes the best biscuit, Rabbi.

ROSE: So? Why shouldn't I make a good biscuit, Rabbi?

RABBI: *(Munching)* The best, Rose. 'S a good biscuit, a fine biscuit.*(They all munch)*

104

(Door bursts open and in stamps the guards' machinegun squad. Many shots outside from police, Anarchist groans and running feet)

SERGEANT: Set up the Maxim gun here, Jones!
JONES: Right, Sergeant! *(Heavy-frame tripod effects)*
SERGEANT: MacTavish!
MAC: Sergeant?
SERGEANT: Load up! Range, Johnson?
JOHNSON: Open sights, Sergeant. Point blank.

(More shots. Cries of 'Down with the Tsar!' 'Screw the Royal family!' 'The hell with the Archbishop of Canterbury!'

VOICE: *(Outside, after hansom cab arrives)* Ah, Captain! How are things going? *(It's the voice of Churchill as a young man)*
CAPTAIN: Quite well, sir.
CHURCHILL: You've done well, Captain. Is there a machinegun set up in case they make a break for it?
CAPTAIN: Over in that house, sir. The Maxim will open fire if they try and leave, sir.
CHURCHILL: Good. I'll go and see for myself.

(Knock on door. Many shots, etc.)

MAURICE: Come!

(Door opens. Enter feet)

CHURCHILL: Good morning. May I come in?
MAURICE: Come! Like a glass lemon tea?
CHURCHILL: Thank you, most kind!
ROSE: 'Ave a biscuit. Enjoy!
CHURCHILL: Thank you, ma'am. *(Munches)* Delicious. Home-made, ma'am?
SID: Rose makes a fine biscuit.
SAM: Such a biscuit. *(They all munch)*
CHURCHILL: You do indeed, ma'am. Sergeant!
SERGEANT: *(Stamps to attention)* Sah!
CHURCHILL: Anything new I should know about?
ROSE: The sink's blocked again.
MAURICE: Yes, the sink's blocked again.
CHURCHILL: Probably the tea leaves.
SID: That's what I said – the tea leaves.

SAM: I said that – the tea leaves.

IZZY: Yes, it's probably the tea leaves.

RABBI: Yes, I'm sure it's the tea leaves.

CHURCHILL: Most probably, Rabbi. Mrs Churchill often says so. 'It's the tea leaves,' she says. Blocks the sink, you know.

SERGEANT: They're moving, sir. *(Shots, yells)*

CHURCHILL: Open fire!

(The house reverberates to the sound of the Maxim gun. Yells from street, groans, shots, explosions and big fire crackling, charging feet, ancient fire brigade and horses)

CHURCHILL: *(Munching)* I say, these really are good biscuits. I must tell Clementine.

(Music up and out)

The short, sharp 'blackout' type of sketch was for years the working basis of revues. The thirties saw many splendid examples of this type of entertainment, such as the C. B. Cochran Revues, the Fargeon shows and the Crazy Gang at the London Palladium.

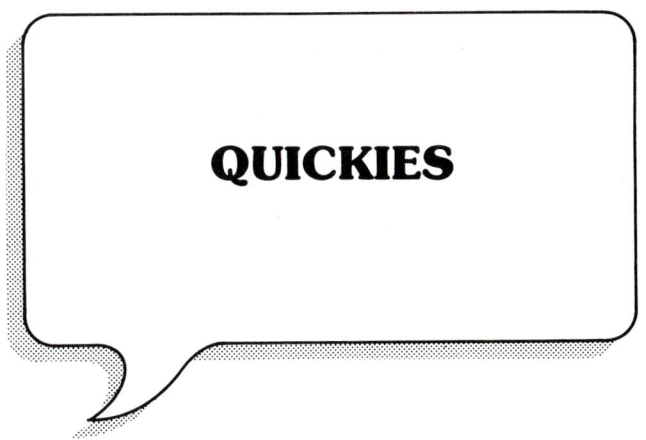

QUICKIES

The war years produced little that was new, except on radio, and once the blitz of London had ended the sort of entertainment handed out to the leave-hungry Allied troops was thin wartime gruel sprinkled with such leggy chorus girls as had managed to stay out of the forces.

It was then that Sid Field – a traditional touring comedian with a marvellously appealing personality – suddenly appeared in the West End and the sketch type of revue material happily returned to the London scene.

'Quickies' reappeared, and as the post-war years took over with their lavish American musicals, the short 'blackout' revues became the cheaper alternative. This type of sketch depends on a shock ending and is best written backwards. Start with the tag, which must be strong, and then work up the premise and the characters to establish the situation.

A lot of television comedy writers today deal in situation comedy, where the laughter is pre-recorded and then afterwards played into the show. Their attitude is often based on the belief that no sketch needs a tag. Using this argument, neither does a funny story, which I find hard to believe.

Those contemplating becoming comedy writers should start with the 'blackout' type of material. Simply stated, this is roughly:

(1) The 'set-up'. The scene, the characters and the motif.
(2) The 'come-on'. The build-up to the climax, with as authentic an atmosphere as possible, and finally
(3) The 'sting'. The tag which you hope will get the belly laugh.

It is the essence of all 'sight' comedy, the backbone of radio and the indispensable ingredient of the great short story.

VIP VISIT

A corner of a television studio. The presenter is standing in front of Camera One.

PRESENTER: Hello! And a very warm welcome to the show! We have a most exciting line-up for you tonight . . .

He is interrupted by a loud voice and into the studio streams a small crowd of guests dressed in the usual wardrobe assistant's idea of 'national' costume. Among them we see a Turk, an Egyptian, a Russian, a German, a Frenchman and an Italian.
  Leading the posse of visitors is a pompous, self-important BBC official, completely oblivious of the fact that he has barged in on a live show.

OFFICIAL: *(Loudly)* Now, here is one of our smaller studios, where we telerecord the *less* important shows. However, as you can see, it is fully equipped with lighting, microphones, scenery and actors. *(He casually directs the interested guests' attention towards each item. The Presenter is standing in respectful silence while he does so)*

OFFICIAL: As you can appreciate, we have to be professional even with our minor shows. Now, are there any questions? *(He looks smugly at his visitors)*

EGYPTIAN: *(Diffidently)* Excuse me, effendi, but what is the significance of the little red light on top of the camera which is shining so brightly? *(He points towards the camera)*

OFFICIAL: *(Relieved that the question is an easy one)* Ah! Yes, indeed! That little red light indicates that the camera is live. That is to say, at this moment the camera is operating and the show is being transmitted . . . *(Realization hits)* Jesus Christ! *(He hurls himself flat on the floor, urgently motioning the others to do the same. Led by the crawling official, they wriggle their way out of shot)*

PRESENTER: As I was saying: Welcome to the show!

DINGLEWEED

A typical set for Gardener's World *or* Horticultural Hour. *A table is set with three small box trays and a sign reading 'Dingleweed'. Behind the table stands the Expert, a weatherbeaten son of the soil, with accent to match.*

EXPERT: I'm going to show you a new Rotational crop, what has been developed by the Ministry for Small Holdings and Market Gardens. It is called 'Dingleweed' and is a very interesting development. Very interesting indeed. Now, this is a young Dingleweed. *(He points to the first wooden box tray)* As you can see, it is quite a sensitive plant when young and, therefore, it 'as to be protected from the harmful ultra-voilet rays of the sun. This is done by placing a thick woven matting between the sun's rays and the young Dingleweed. *(He does so, putting a small foot-square section of woven string-mat on top of four short bamboo sticks which are set at the four corners of the box tray)* Now, then – there we have the sensitive young Dingleweed noicely pertected from the harmful ultra-voilet rays of the sun.

(The Expert indicates the second box tray, which contains a two-foot-high Dingleweed with a thick stem and a broccoli-type top)

EXPERT: When the Dingleweed is a year old, it has developed its own ultra-voilet pertection from the harmful rays of the sun and has developed into a hardy plant – which is ready for harvesting.

(The Expert harvests it by pulling it up by its roots)

EXPERT: At this toime of the year, the Dingleweed harvesters go out into the Dingleweed fields, for it is Dingleberry toime. *(He shows that under the foliage at the top of the plant is a small bunch of orange-coloured berries)* These are, of course, the seed-berries from which the next crop of Dingleweed will be grown.

(The Expert lays the Dingleweed out on the table and attacks it with a mallet)

EXPERT: The next step after gatherin' in the Dingleweed harvest is to slub it and groin it. *(He slubs it with the mallet and then stretches the twisted stringy fibres in his hands)* A groinin' fork is used to groin the Dingleweed. *(He groins it with the groinin' fork)* Then for two weeks the Dingleweed is soaked in a mixture of honey-molasses and cod-liver oil, until it is noice and ploiable. *(He ploies it about noicely)* Then it is allowed to dry out in the sun, until it is finally ready for making into the end product. *(With a flourish, the Expert picks up the end product)* It is woven into this thick matting, which is used to pertect the young Dingleweed from the harmful ultra-voilet rays of the sun.

ÊTRE – TO BE, A FRENCH TRAGEDY

This quickie is an example of how sexy the French language can be.

A schoolmaster, in traditional gown and mortar-board, stands in front of a blackboard and uses a pointer to explain to the viewers or theatre audience the significance of the great French verb – Être.

SCHOOLMASTER: *(primly)* Être – to be.

Je suis	*I* am
tu es	*thou* art
il est	*he* is
nous sommes	*we* are
vous êtes	*you* are
ils sont	*they* are

Par exemple!

(Sexy French accordion music is used as the background atmosphere for this section of a small French apartment. A couch dominates the scene, with the back towards the audience, concealing the action taking place upon it. (For radio, the scene is set with music and creaking bedsprings) Just above the back of the couch we see the tops of the heads of a man and woman close together. Springs creak in the couch, music continues and loud, sexy kissing sounds are heard)

MAN'S VOICE: *(Panting)* Oh! Oh! *Je suis!*
WOMAN'S VOICE: *(Equally excited)* Oh! *Tu es!*

(Sound of heavy boots outside as the front door below opens and slams shut, followed by the booted feet coming up the long wooden staircase. NB: In radio, or sound effects off-stage, all staircases are wooden)

WOMAN: *(Her head and naked shoulders appearing as she sits up in alarm)* Oh! *Il est!*
MAN: *(Also appearing with naked shoulders and Gallicly indicating their naked state with his hands)* Et – *nous sommes!*
WOMAN: *(Terrified and pointing to his lower half)* Et – *vous êtes!*

(The door bursts open and into the room crashes a large bereted and trenchcoated Frenchman – his face a mask of jealous fury)

CUCKOLDED FRENCHMAN: Agh! Mon Dieu! *Ils sont!*

(He pulls out a revolver and shoots them both)

THE HOBBYIST

PRESENTER: At this point in our show tonight I should like to introduce
you to a man who, for my money, is one of the finest hobby craftsmen

that I have ever come across. Mortimer Brinsley is a bank clerk, but his first love is the skilled use of his hands. Mortimer is a model-maker specializing in architectural models, and tonight he has brought along his superb model of St Paul's Cathedral.

This magnificent example of British amateur craftsmanship has taken Mortimer ten years to complete and his four-foot-high wooden model of St Paul's Cathedral stands as a mute witness to those ten years of devoted effort! Incidentally, Mortimer Brinsley's model of St Paul's is made entirely out of three million matches.

(As the Presenter turns to beckon the great British hobbyist on to the stage there is a dull explosion and a large mushroom of smoke rises into view from the wings at the side of the stage)

PRESENTER: Mr Mortimer Brinsley! Oh! Ah, yes!

(Onto the stage comes Mortimer. His scorched suit, singed hair and smudged and blackened face emphasize the disaster. He carries in front of him a flat tray on which a stumpy heap of burnt matches is still smouldering. He stands beside the Presenter in mute misery)

PRESENTER: *(Cheerfully)* Well, Mortimer! Perhaps you could come back? In . . . *(Pause)* . . . about ten years' time?

CRICKET

Once again this is primarily a radio piece, but it can equally well work on television or stage with only the Commentator in vision, sitting in a Commentator's box with his microphone in front of him.

(Crowd effects of a quiet, well-behaved type)

COMMENTATOR: The whole match could well be decided in the next over with this change of bowling. Ted Dowling is new to first class cricket, but he is a bowler to watch. There he goes, taking that characteristically long walk of his back from the wicket. Ted really likes to get a bit of distance between himself and the wicket. Yes, there he goes!

(Over this commentary we hear Ted walk heavily back over the turf, passing through the little gate set in the wooden paling fence, up the wooden steps, through a door, across the hollow echoing boards of the pavilion floor, out through the front door and finally walking down some stone steps on to the pavement outside the cricket ground)

TED'S VOICE: *(In the distance)* Taxi!

(Taxi stops. The door opens and shuts and the cab speeds up the road, stopping with a screech of brakes. Now in quick succession we hear the following:

(1)   The cab door opens

(2)   Footsteps run down the road back towards the cricket ground

(3)   Ted runs up the stone steps of the pavilion

(4)   The pavilion outer door opens and shuts

(5)   Ted runs across the echoing wooden pavilion floor

(6)   The door to the cricket ground opens and shuts with more running down the wooden steps

(7)   The wooden gate opens and shuts

(8)   Footsteps accelerate across the grass

(9)   A terrific effort from Ted as he bowls

(10) A gasp from the crowd)

UMPIRE: No ball!

The more espionage novels I read the more I realize that, with some notable exceptions, few of the authors know anything about the subject. Apart from the fact that clandestine operations are the dirtiest game in the world, most of an agent's time is spent in study and information gathering.

THE MASTER SPY

A photographic memory is of course an invaluable aid, and most top agents have been trained to 'hone' these abilities to a fine edge. I have known operatives who could scan and digest a page of data-packed typescript in under thirty seconds. They then retained this information in their memories for days and could repeat it verbatim, complete with intricate formulae, until they virtually cleared their inner memory banks and digested the next set of information.

I have good recall, but not total recall, from my own memory banks, but as age takes its toll of my brain cells, my mind is nowhere near as retentive as it was during the Second World War.

This sketch recalls things long past and I wrote it while recovering from a near-fatal pulmonary embolism in 1960.

A darkened room, almost bare of furniture, except for a plain wooden table and a chair. The room is shut off from the outside world by a closed venetian blind. A glass and a carafe of water are on the table. It is a secret rendezvous in some almost deserted neighbourhood, somewhere in the West. The 'spy' as popularly depicted in contemporary novels, is seated behind the table – dimly seen in the subdued light. On the table in front of him are a number of intriguing packages. He wears a dirty trenchcoat.

Dominating the scene is a second man, wearing a close-buttoned and belted leather version of his colleague's 'trench'. He also wears a Trilby hat of sombre hue, with the brim turned down all round. His metal-rimmed glasses and trim 'Lenin' beard are in keeping with his Gestapo-KGB image. He is the Spy Master.

SPY MASTER: The packages on the table in front of you contain the vital information you will require for this mission. I want you to memorize every detail of their contents. Photograph them indelibly on your

memory and then . . . *(He leans forward and almost whispers the next words)* . . . destroy them! You understand, X7?

(The Spy, who never speaks, nods his head grimly)

SPY MASTER: When you have finished impressing all the details on your memory and have destroyed the contents, I will require you to repeat them. You understand, X7?

(Once more he leans close to X7's ear to stage-whisper the last words. The spy nods his head with a curt, decisive movement, then fixes his attention on the first package, which is an envelope)

SPY MASTER: The envelope contains the passport that your target will be carrying. I want you to memorize its contents – impress it photographically on your memory, and then . . . *(He leans forward with a hissing whisper)* . . . destroy it! Understand, X7?

(X7 nods and without any change in his inscrutable visage he opens the envelope, extracts a passport from it, quickly turning over each page after an instant's close inspection. He leafs through the cardboard-bound document and at the end he nods to indicate the completion of his inspection and his memory retention)

SPY MASTER: Excellent, X7. Now destroy it! *(The Master breathes his instructions in his operative's earhole)*

(The spy pulls out a large 'Zippo-type' lighter and spins the wheel to light it, but the Spy Master clamps his hand over the operative's)

SPY MASTER: *(Furiously and vehemently hoarse, as he whispers throatily)* Are you mad, X7? No lights! *They* are watching our every move. *(He leans right up to X7's ear and grates out breathily)* Destroy it!

(X7 looks slightly nonplussed. Then it slowly dawns on him that he will have to eat the documents. There is no other way to be rid of them)

SPY MASTER: *(As his operative hesitates)* Destroy it! *(His tone brooks no delay)*

(X7 deliberately tears up the passport and eats it from cover to cover, chewing each piece and page and swallowing with considerable effort. (On radio we use the sound effects to convey the illusion, which can be even more effective in the mind of the listener.) As soon as X7 has finished and swallowed the last fragment of the passport, he takes a drink of water and looks up expectantly at his Spy Master)

SPY MASTER: *(Taking a rolled-up package from the table and unrolling it into a fair-sized chart)* Here is the plan of the rocket firing-range where the new top-secret missile is stored.

(X7 stares in disbelief at the size of the chart he will eventually have to swallow, but being highly trained he closely examines its detail)

SPY MASTER: *(As a leit-motif while his operative is at work)* Examine it closely! Photograph every detail in your memory and then . . . *(Again the close vindictive whisper)* . . . destroy it!

(X7 does so – scanning the chart at close quarters, blinking one eye like the shutter of a camera. Then, with only a short hesitation, he tears it up and stuffs it into his mouth – chewing away, swallowing it all and finally drinking another glass of water. (Note: Of course, everything is made of wafer-thin pastry and rice paper, dyed with vegetable colouring, but it still requires quite a physical effort to eat and

swallow the amount of 'documentation' required.) While X7 is still swallowing his chart entrée, the Spy Master has handed him a small packet which X7 unrolls to reveal a 16mm strip of black and white film negative – made of gelatine)

SPY MASTER: This microfilm shows the control mechanism of the new missile. Memorize it! Photograph the details indelibly on your memory – and then repeat it all! Excellent!

(The Spy Master obviously approves the efficient way in which X7 has unrolled the narrow film strip to its full length of two feet and is now holding it close up to his 'camera lens' left eye, while he blinks away at each separate picture and moves the strip rapidly past his eyeline)

SPY MASTER: Destroy it!

(X7 does so, quite enjoying its gelatine flavour and chewing away with pleasure. He swallows the microfilm down with a hearty swig of water. As he licks his lips and picks his teeth, the Spy Master produces a large rectangular wooden box and places it in front of X7)

SPY MASTER: This is a scale model of their new missile. The deadly orbital global range FU-2.

(Before the Spy Master can stop him, X7 has grabbed the box and has bitten a large lump of 'wood' out of the lid. The Spy Master snatches the box away)

SPY MASTER: *(Furiously)* Not the box! The *contents* of the box are top secret!

(The box lid has a shortbread insert and X7 is now chewing this with obvious enjoyment. He looks apprehensively at the rocket missile which the Spy Master is holding. It is about a foot long and two inches in diameter – hollow – but made out of marzipan, with the tail fins fashioned from wafer biscuits. When coloured with food dye it looks splendidly authentic)

SPY MASTER: Examine it closely! *(X7 does so)* Photograph it in your mind! *(X7 does this as well)* and now . . . *(Pauses dramatically with his head close to X7)* . . . destroy it!

(X7 chews off large chunks of his 'dessert' rocket and, masticating madly, finishes off with heavy efforts at swallowing – washed down with the last of the carafe of water. He is at the end of his tether)

SPY MASTER: Now, X7, have you examined every detail of this Top Secret information?

(X7 nods wearily)

SPY MASTER: Have you photographed every single detail in your memory files?

(X7 nods again)

SPY MASTER: There remains only one thing more for you to do . . . *(Pauses dramatically – savouring the moment)* Now X7! Repeat it!

(X7 nods and BURPS an enormous, endless BELCH)

Since the end of the Second World War, the 'mysterious island people of Japan', as the pre-war travelogues described them, have become quite familiar in the West.

A marvellous caption to the famous 'surrender' picture of the Japanese commanding General handing over his Samurai sword to General MacArthur, bore the words: 'What the hell, there's always transistors.' Japan has flooded the West with cars, motorcycles, television sets, radios, Hi-Fis, matchless cameras and optical goods, thus exacting an incredible peacetime economic revenge for their ignominious wartime defeat.

But the Japan that still captures the imagination is that of the Geisha and the Tea Ceremony, the martial arts and those delightful miniature gardens, with their Bonzai trees and tiny earthenware figures and temples. These next pieces are about this image of Japan.

DIGITZU, NO-KENDO AND THE JAPANESE BEETLE

THE MARTIAL ARTS

Two Japanese practitioners of the great martial arts stand in front of a screened window. They are dressed in loose judo-style jackets and trousers and have large heraldic symbols on the back of their clothes. In front of them stands the martial arts master, in an impressive black version of the same costume, holding his Samurai sword at his side. Beside him stands Clyde Quigley, the American Interviewer. He addresses his audience.

CLYDE: Tonight we are about to learn the secrets of two of Japan's greatest martial arts. Beside me is Professor Oshito Yokimotza, one of Japan's foremost exponents of the dual arts of the murderous martial sports of Digitzu and No-Kendo! Firstly what is Digitzu, Professor? *(He turns enquiringly, fixing the great martial arts master with a piercing glare)*

YOKIMOTZA: *(in Japanese accent and intonation)* Digitzu is very old Japanese method of self-defence, teaching muscular control of whole body, building indomitable will and self control – and, incidentally, it is excellent in severe cases of constipation.

CLYDE: Fascinating! What parts of the body are used most in this murderously dangerous martial art?

YOKIMOTZA: The forefinger!

(He holds up his own forefinger, which is about twice as long as normal and obviously lethally strong)

CLYDE: The forefinger? *(He turns and addresses the audience)* The mind boggles at the damage such a forefinger could do!

YOKIMOTZA: True! Behind me are Mikimoto Havabasha, Yokohama's reigning Digitzu Champion . . . *(The indicated expert bows low)* . . . and his Digitzu instructor, Sakaru Notatossa, an eminent Yokohama physician, surgeon and flower arranger. *(The distinguished doctor also bows)*

CLYDE: *(Bowing back awkwardly)* They just fight with their forefingers?

YOKIMOTZA: That is correct. But Digitzu is no ordinary martial art. It requires many more years of intensive and demanding training. So!

(He indicates a side table on which stand three bowls. Havabasha takes position behind them with his long forefinger raised ready to strike)

YOKIMOTZA: For two years Digitzu student sticks his finger into cold rice pudding. *(With a sudden cry, Havabasha does so)* This hardens the finger and also finds a use for cold rice pudding. Now Digitzu student shoves his finger into stale Madeira cake – for one year. *(Havabasha plunges his forefinger into the second bowl amid a shower of crumbs)*

YOKIMOTZA: And lastly for one month only Digitzu student finishes off this finger-hardening process by sticking his forefinger into bowl of broken dog biscuits. *(Havabasha obliges with a short martial bark)*

YOKIMOTZA: This finally produces the desired effect for the Digitzu student, who now becomes the proud possessor of a Number One rigid digit.

(Havabasha proudly sticks his finger into the air)

CLYDE: A deadly weapon in the right hands!

YOKIMOTZA: Precisely! Also in the left hands.

CLYDE: How does a Digitzu master use his rigid digit?

YOKIMOTZA: Sparingly! Once Digitzu student becomes possessor of rigid digit he has to carry finger licence. All Japanese Digitzu masters are known to the police and duly licensed to carry hardened forefinger.

CLYDE: How many are there?

YOKIMOTZA: Forefingers?

CLYDE: Licensed Digitzu masters.

YOKIMOTZA: Three.

CLYDE: Three?

YOKIMOTZA: Three. These two and humble self – ah-so!

CLYDE: Incredible!

YOKIMOTZA: But true. The three main attack positions with Digitzu forefinger are: One! Mince Piezu!

(Havabasha with a yell of 'U-Basta!' sticks Dr Notatossa in the eye – neatly parried by the doctor's own forefinger)

YOKIMOTZA: Two! Up-Hoota!

(Havabasha obliges by sticking his rigid digit up the doctor's left nostril)

HAVABASHA: U-Kleep!

(The doctor shakes his head as he parries deftly)

YOKIMOTZA: And three! Gobitzu!

(The doctor leaps behind Havabasha and sticks both forefingers, left and right, into Havabasha's mouth and widens his lips into an enormous smile. Havabasha sticks

121

his forefinger behind him into the doctor's hidden lower half and with a grunt of agony the crippled physician lets go. Finally they both bow low)

CLYDE: Could we see a bout?
YOKIMOTZA: Certainly. On guard!

(The two Digitzu masters cautiously spar – their forefingers held like swords – until, with a brief flurry of action, the doctor obviously gives Havabasha a hearty 'goose'! His opponent screams and crashes sideways through the paper and wooden slat-covered window)

CLYDE: Most exciting! Is Dr Notatossa famous in Japan?
YOKIMOTZA: As Digitzu master, no. As obstetrician, yes!

(Clyde now moves over to a second, smaller set where two Samurai warriors in full traditional armour are standing in their large Samurai boots, holding huge ancient wooden clubs. They are standing at arm's length from each other facing the audience and are raised above the ground, by about three feet, on a rostrum covered in grass matting. They both bow and salute Yokimotza and Clyde with their huge clubs)

YOKIMOTZA: Here are two famous Samurai masters of *other* great Japanese Martial Art, No-Kendo.

CLYDE: I've heard of Kendo. Japanese sword-fighting. But what is No-Kendo?

YOKIMOTZA: No-Kendo come long before Kendo. Invented by the Great Kublai Khan's Uncle, Kublai Khant – No-Kendo.

(They bow as a big gong is sounded)

YOKIMOTZA: Note their crubs.

CLYDE: Crubs?

YOKIMOTZA: *Wooden* crubs. Made of Minge wood. Very ancient. Very heavy. Broody painful. These crubs are soaked for two years in stale seaweed by Yokohama Senior Citizens. This finds use for stale seaweed and give Yokohama Old Age Pensioners something to do – apart from considering voluntary euthanasia. Yet No-Kendo battle commence!

(The gong sounds again and with a loud shout of 'Bonzai' the left-hand Samurai raises his club and, without moving his legs, swings his body round and smites his opponent on the helmet, with a loud crash. His stricken target yells 'Ouch!' and grows shorter by about six inches – his legs disappearing into his large boots, which are hollow and let their wearer slide down on a car-jack which is remotely

controlled off stage. (A beautiful prop, modified for me by that master ex-BBC prop designer, Jack Kine.)

The second Samurai from his lowered position does the same manoeuvre – clobbering his opponent and shortening him by a good six inches as well. The battle continues, with each in turn clubbing his opponent into his boots, until they both stop, each of them about two feet shorter than when they started, but still apparently intact – except that their large armoured boots appear to come up to their crutches. They both bow. The gong sounds again)

YOKIMOTZA: Now comes traditional Samurai battle cry!

BOTH SAMURAI: *(Holding their helmeted heads)* Oo, watta basta Bonzai!

YOKIMOTZA: Roughly translated it means 'Have you got a broody aspirin?'

(The Samurai bow from the waist, looking like truncated midgets)

CLYDE: Has this sport been going on for a long time in Japan?

YOKIMOTZA: Naturally! That is why Japanese people a rittle short!

THE KAMIKAZE BEETLE

I have included this sketch because I've done it on stage and television in a number of countries and, like my Flea Circus of Invisible Fleas, it is a great favourite of mine, mainly because the models have been made so beautifully.

INTERVIEWER: *(Earnestly)* When I was a boy one of my greatest pleasures was building up one of those charming little table-top Japanese gardens, filled with miniature cacti and a small Bonzai tree. The little figurines, model bridges and temples were delightfully attractive and the whole effect most pleasing. Since the end of the war, these little Japanese gardens have virtually disappeared. In the studio tonight we have a Japanese gardening expert, Dr Mishimoto Bangamashi of the Imperial School of Miniature Gardening and Brain Surgery. Good evening, doctor. Can you tell us why Japanese miniature gardens seem to have declined in Occidental popularity?

BANGAMASHI: *(Bowing low)* Certainly! All due to depredations of dreaded Kamikaze beetle. Japanese miniature garden need Bonzai tree. Bonzai tree very old. Kamikaze beetle eat Bonzai tree in few seconds. No Bonzai tree, no Japanese garden! Kamikaze beetle little sod!

INTERVIEWER: Quite so! How terrible!

BANGAMASHI: Please to come with me. *(They walk over to a table on which is a two-foot-long tray, with all the traditional bits and pieces associated with these gardens)*

INTERVIEWER: Enchanting!

BANGAMASHI: Indeed! See, Bonzai tree very fine example of miniature Japanese oak, two hundred years old, also pagoda and small summer pavilion garden house and also Japanese sage by bridge, here. *(Indicates the bridge)*

INTERVIEWER: Is that sage like our herb?

BANGAMASHI: Don't know what your friend Herb look like. *This* sage is wise-man-type sage. *(Indicates the venerable mini-figure)*

INTERVIEWER: *(Covering up)* Ah, quite so!

BANGAMASHI: Also small pine trees, ferns, cacti, rittle garden ornaments and fisherman fishing by rittle pond.

INTERVIEWER: What is the sandy strip for in front? It looks a bit stark.

BANGAMASHI: That not stark strip. That take-off strip for Kamikaze beetle. *(He produces a small circular pill box)* Here is Kamikaze beetle.

(He opens the box to show invisible beetle buzzing about inside the box. This is done with a miniature vibrator which rapidly oscillates a thin rubber diaphragm (actually a contraceptive) which is stretched inside the box and is covered with fuller's earth. As the buzzer vibrates, the dust shoots up and down very impressively)

BANGAMASHI: *(Taking invisible beetle between forefinger and thumb)* I now prace Kamikaze beetle on end of take-off strip. *(He does so)* Note energetic use of Kamikaze's wings!

(We see a cloud of dust blown back from the end of the sandy strip and the Kamikaze beetle apparently takes off. This is accomplished by the combined illusion of four spaced-out spring-operated piano hammers, which, when released, cause the sand to jump, as though the beetle is hopping along, plus the sounds of beetle-style 'revving' and a typical much-speeded-up jet plane taking off)

INTERVIEWER: What now?

BANGAMASHI: Kamikaze having taken off from the sandy strip . . . *(The two small pine trees at the end of the runway wag about as the beetle zooms past them)* . . . he now climbs to cruising height above target area – Japanese miniature Bonzai tree! So! *(Indicating beetle flight-path above his head)* Kamikaze beetle reaches cruising altitude. Soon he attack Bonzai tree.

INTERVIEWER: Can't ordinary pesticides and sprays deal with this beetle?

BANGAMASHI: We have tried everything. Please observe! *(Picks up a fly-spray can and sprays the area above him)* Ordinary spray have rittle effect on Kamikaze beetle *(Slight coughing and a spit illustrates how 'rittle' the effect is)*

INTERVIEWER: Incredible!

(The tone of the bomber-like buzzing changes to one of a diving Stuka)

BANGAMASHI: Ah! Kamikaze beetle commence attack dive on to Bonzai tree!

(His head and the Interviewer's eyeline follow the beetle down as the mini dive-bombing whine increases in volume, then abruptly stops, as the beetle lands on a Bonzai tree branch, which immediately bends with a 'boing' effect)

BANGAMASHI: Kamikaze beetle has landed! Observe amazing appetite of Kamikaze beetle!

(A speeded-up munching sound is heard and the Kamikaze beetle apparently eats all the foliage off the little tree. This effect is accomplished by the tree and its branches being hollow. Through them are threaded strong nylon threads, decorated at the end with large brightly-coloured sea ferns and parrot feathers. The nylon threads are all attached together under the trunk of the Bonzai tree and bound to strong catapult elastic, secured by a pin – so, when the pin is withdrawn, the nylon threads are

126

pulled sharply away and the 'foliage' disappears down each branch of the tree at the same time. As the feathers and ferns are sprinkled with fuller's earth, the effect is instant, effective and startling. At the same time, we hear mini-sound effects of the beetle swallowing followed by a mini-burp)

INTERVIEWER: How terrible!

BANGAMASHI: Terrible and terminal! Bonzai tree now destroyed! *(Shouts)* TIMBER!

(The Bonzai tree creaks over and – to the sound of an actual giant redwood falling – crashes down on the garden)

INTERVIEWER: Tragic!

(The beetle makes a drunken buzzing sound and leaves the tree, which is now lying on its side. The branch on which it has been sitting 'poings' back as the beetle takes off, with its beetle-motor now sounding hesitant, with mini-belches, and rather slow in tempo. Obviously the beetle has eaten too much)

BANGAMASHI: *Now* is psychological moment to attack beetle. Japanese people very ingenious people, so have developed effective anti-Kamikaze beetle techniques. Observe please, Japanese garden house pavilion.

(As the beetle drunkenly climbs to its cruising height, the pavilion opens its roof and through it appears a radar-dish aerial, together with the accepted but inaccurate sonar 'pinging' sound. The antenna rotates)

BANGAMASHI: Anti-Kamikaze radar picks up 'blip' of beetle. Now Japanese anti-aircraft garden battery come into action!

(The pagoda falls apart to reveal a concealed twin-barrelled anti-aircraft gun, which commences firing. The two barrels alternately recoil and smoke shoots from each muzzle – while the sound of twin Oerlikon cannons accompanies the action)

BANGAMASHI: A direct hit!

(The Kamikaze beetle sound is drowned out by the explosion of the shells above the garden. The Interviewer and the good doctor both use their eyelines to show where the beetle is hovering)

BANGAMASHI: We got him!

(The beetle noise turns into the rising whine of a crashing plane and Bangamashi and the Interviewer follow the spinning dive of the invisible beetle till it crashes

through the small bridge into the pond, from which a spout of water is blown up as a loud splash is heard)

BANGAMASHI: *(Looks up at the camera and smiles inscrutably)* Kamikaze beetle has committed insecticide! Ah, so! *(Bows)*

A wave of violent crime seemed at one time to be concentrated on small village post offices. These are usually a part of a small store or village shop which sells everything from a needle to an anchor. In a number of cases of village post office hold-ups, the postmasters and even postmistresses unexpectedly fought back and the crime wave receded as the villains sought easier pickings.

Here is my tribute to those gallant souls who refused to be intimidated by armed cowards.

THE HOLD-UP

A typical village store/cum post office. The main part of the little shop is taken up by a counter, with brass weights on it, and an old-fashioned weighing machine, large country cheeses under glass, a home-cooked ham covered with gauze which is weighted down by glass beads, and shelves filled to sagging with tins and bottles of all kinds.

In front of the counter are large tins of biscuits and sacks of potatoes, while salamis and onion-strings hang from the ceiling. Only a very small part of this establishment is set aside for the post office, with its posters and notices, mostly yellow with age and long out of date.

The whole shop should give off an aura of boot-polish, madeira cake, beeswax and liniment. (This is difficult on television.) It is the centre of the rural community.

Mr Sloggett, the proprietor, in shirt-sleeves and a spotless apron, is deferentially looking after the Squire, an ancient local aristocrat.

SLOGGETT: Now, Squire. Try a bit of this Stilton.
SQUIRE: *(While doing so and munching away mutters inaudibly)* Cheese – pipe – Bombay – large woman – gurkhas – Indian mutiny –*(chuckles)* Poona – passion – fruit – killed him! Not bad! The cheese.
SLOGGETT: Try a little bit of local cheddar. *Gorge*-ous, if you get my meaning, Squire? *Cheddar gorge-ous!*
SQUIRE: *(Munches cheddar)* Excellent. Very good, Sloggett. *(Chuckles)* Reminds me. Singapore – torrential downpour – huge woman – general's ADC – AC/DC – I/C – in an upturned rickshaw – bright green – belly dancer – *huge* – stone dead! *(Finishes eating)*

SLOGGETT: Shall I send some cheese up to the manor, Squire? About two pounds?

SQUIRE: *(Vaguely)* No, thank ye, Sloggett. I've had quite enough. Very tasty! *(Exits, still reminiscing about the Far East)* Darjeeling – young Smithers – pet ostrich – deeply in love – family refused. Shot the ostrich! Then himself. Tragedy!

(The shop-bell tinkles as the Squire shambles out into the street. Phone rings. Sloggett answers it)

SLOGGETT: Yes, Mrs 'Umblebottom. A *very* nice day! No, we 'aven't got pickled humming birds. But we just got in some nice tinned chicken. Good! I'll send some up with the usual groceries this morning. My lad's on holiday, so I'll pop 'em up meself. Goodbye, Mrs 'Umble-bottom.

(As he replaces the old two-piece receiver on the telephone, the door-bell tinkles and a rain-coated figure enters, with a stocking-mask over his head. He takes out a revolver from a carrier bag and points it at Sloggett)

SLOGGETT: *(Politely)* Yes, sir? Good mornin', and what may I do for you today?

GUNMAN: Dis is a stick-up. Hand over de money! *(He extends the paper carrier)*

SLOGGETT: *(Unmoved)* Yes, sir. Certainly, sir. *(Goes to cash register)* I hope you don't mind, most of it is change? I've got to go to the bank and I haven't made it up yet.

GUNMAN: Just hand it over! Quick, moind!

SLOGGETT: *(Taking handfuls of coins – silver and bronze – from the till and a few pound notes and stuffing them into the ancient paper carrier, which bursts, showering coins all over the counter)* Them paper carriers never do hold very much. I'll get you a box.

GUNMAN: *(Suspiciously)* No tricks, moind.

SLOGGETT: Oh no, sir. It'll be just an *ordinary* box, sir. Nothin' fancy. Ah! *(Finds one)* This'll do nicely. *(He sweeps all the coins together and then pauses)* Perhaps you'd like the coins separate in a plastic carrier? And *then* put 'em in the box, sir?

GUNMAN: Oh! Yus, orlright. But be quick about it! Dis gun is loaded. *(He pulls the trigger. Nothing happens)* Oh! I remember I only got two bullets. *(Opens the cylinder of the revolver and spins it)* 'Ang on! Dat's better. *(Levels it again)* Now get a move on – or I'll blow yer 'ead orf!

SLOGGETT: *(Still cool)* Right, sir. There we are. Loose change – about five pounds worth – in the liddle plastic carrier bag and four pounds in notes, all in the box. Let's see, that'll be sixpence.

GUNMAN: What for?

SLOGGETT: The carrier bag. The paper ones are fourpence and the strong plastic ones are sixpence.

GUNMAN: *(Hypnotized by Sloggett's calm rustic assurance)* Oh, right. *(He takes a sixpenny piece – which shows you how long ago I wrote this sketch – and gives it to Sloggett, who rings it up on the ancient cash register)*

GUNMAN: Now! De post office takings.

SLOGGETT: Certainly, sir. Over 'ere, if you please. *(Sloggett slips two black over-sleeves on to his arms and puts on a green eye-shade. He is now standing behind the little wire-grilled post office counter)*

SLOGGETT: Now, sir, what can the post office do for you, sir?

GUNMAN: 'And over the money! Everyfink! *(He points the gun menacingly at the shopman)*

SLOGGETT: *(Opening the post office drawer and extracting some notes)* As it's Saturday, there's not much, I'm sorry to say. About three pounds in notes and two pounds in change.

GUNMAN: Postal orders?

SLOGGETT: Oh yes! There's a few of them.

GUNMAN: 'And 'em over!

SLOGGETT: *(Doing so)* Stamps?

GUNMAN: Yes.

SLOGGETT: 'Ow many?

GUNMAN: *(Thinks)* Oh! Let's see, abaht two dozen tuppennies and a couple of dozen pennies. Oh, and 'ave you got them new Coronation ones? The bigguns. *(Which really shows how long ago this sketch was originally conceived)*

SLOGGETT: I have got a few left. Been a big run on 'em, sir. Ah yes! I just got three left. There we are! *(He adds them to the small pile of notes and coins on the counter and pushes the whole lot through the grille-opening)*

GUNMAN: Ta! *(Shovels it all into the cardboard box)*

(The phone rings. Sloggett doesn't quite know what to do)

GUNMAN: Answer it! No tricks now!

SLOGGETT: Right, sir. *(Picks up phone)* 'Allo. Sloggett's Emporium. Mr Sloggett speaking. Oh! It's *you* again, Mrs 'Umblebottom. No, I didn't take your weekend order. *(He clamps one hand over the mouthpiece)* It's Mrs 'Umblebottom with 'er weekend order.

GUNMAN: Take it down! Don't try anyfink funny!

SLOGGETT: Right, Mrs 'Umblebottom. Fire away *(Clamps hand hurriedly over telephone)* Not you, sir. *(Takes hand away)* Yes, ma'am. A packet of dried peas. *(Reaches down and puts the packet on the counter into another large cardboard box)* Two tins of plums. *(Finds them and pops them into the box)* A bag of self-raising flour. *(Reaches for that and boxes it)* Two pounds of Garibaldi biscuits – just a moment! *(To gunman)* I can't reach. Do you mind? *(Indicates biscuit boxes)*

GUNMAN: No. *(Reaches down)* Orlright.

SLOGGETT: Garibaldis – *them* there!

(Gunman finds the biscuits and hands them over)

SLOGGETT: *(To phone)* Right, ma'am. A quart of cider, semi-sweet, and a bottle of gin. *(To gunman)* Would you oblige me, sir? Over there! *(Indicates their whereabouts)*

GUNMAN: *(Completely mesmerized)* 'Ere? Right! *(He locates the bottles and hands them over)* Anyfink else?

SLOGGETT: Anything else, Mrs 'Umblebottom? Oh yes! A packet of pins. Two pounds of best cheddar. *(To gunman)* Would you mind cutting off a chunk? *(Indicates how much on the large cheese block)* About there! Don't cut yourself! *(Hands the gunman a large knife)* A pound of coffee. *(Takes down tin from shelf)* A quarter pound of Darjeeling tea. Oh! The Squire must be coming over to tea. A small caraway-seed cake – oh yes, ma'am. The Squire is definitely coming. That's 'is favourite. *(Quickly)* Two smoked pig's trotters. *(To gunman)* 'Anging up there. A new broom. *(To gunman)* Over there, sir. *(Gunman grunts and obliges)* A small string of onions. *(Indicates where they are)*

GUNMAN: 'Ere! *(Loads everything into the box on the counter)* 'Urry up! I've got a train to catch.

SLOGGETT: Right, sir. Anything else, Mrs 'Umblebottom? A noggin of nails, two threep danglers, a small stuffed aardvark, four goggle-box tops and some wombat polish. Oh, and worm powders for Cecily. Right! I'll 'ave all that up to Rose Cottage in a jiffy. Bye, Mrs 'Umblebottom.

GUNMAN: You finished?

SLOGGETT: *(Replaces phone)* Yes, sir. Now, what about you, sir? You look a bit over-loaded.

(The gunman has now replaced his revolver in the paper carrier bag and it promptly falls through on to the counter)

SLOGGETT: *(Picking it up and handing it back to the robber)* Careful, sir!

Them things is liable to go off. I tell you what, sir – this lot's a bit awkward for you to carry. Shall I 'ave it delivered?

GUNMAN: *(Now utterly demoralized under the spell of Mr Sloggett's garrulous charm)* Oh! Er – yeah.

SLOGGETT: Where shall I send it? *(Pencil poised)* Sir?

GUNMAN: Sid Burke of no fixed abode. Tell you what, mate. Send it to me addressed to Wormwood Scrubs – HM Prison – I'm bound to be back there soon.

SLOGGETT: *(Making a note of it all)* Certainly, sir. Drop in again, if you're passing.

GUNMAN: *(Making for the door)* Oh, yes. Orlright! How do I get to the station?

SLOGGETT: Turn left out of the door, then straight on to the corner, turn right and at Rose Cottage, that's Mrs 'Umblebottom's home, turn left and it's at the end of the road.

GUNMAN: Oh, ta, mate. Bye. *(Goes to open the shop door. The bell tinkles)* That's pretty. *(The gunman is a very simple soul)*

SLOGGETT: I wonder, as you're passing Rose Cottage, would you be so kind as to pop in these groceries for old Mrs 'Umblebottom? She's not able to get about much.

GUNMAN: *(Who is kind as well as simple)* Oh, orlright, mate. 'Ave I got time? I'm trying to catch the twelve-thirty.

SLOGGETT: *(Loading the gunman up with the heavy box)* Plenty of time, sir. Good day. Nice to 'ave you drop by.

GUNMAN: Oh, ta. Bye, mate. *(He finally exits through the open door, which closes behind him)*

SLOGGETT: *(Going to the phone and banging the receiver up and down)* 'Allo, Mabel. Sloggett 'ere. 'Ere, Mabel, you'll never guess. Get me the p'lice. *(Pause)* I just been robbed!

MABEL: *(Very excited)* Ooh! Alf!

SLOGGETT: 'Allo? Sergeant Bumstead? It's Alf. Alf Sloggett. I just been robbed. Three of 'em. They escaped by car. Took the lot – two hundred pounds from the till and over four hundred pounds from the post office. They'll be miles away by now. All masked – huge men – Irish! I only just managed to untie meself. Yes! I'll report it right away to the Insurance Company. Oh, yes! Right away! Bye, Arthur! *(Replaces receiver)*

(He sucks his pencil and idly jots down some figures)

SLOGGETT: That's six hundred the insurance owes me. *(Pause, and then*

Sloggett rings the telephone operator again) 'Allo, Mabel. 'Allo, darlin'. 'Ow about you and me nippin' across for a cosy weekend in Gay Paree? Eh?

MABEL: Ooh! Alf!

Many years ago the BBC had one of its top commentators stranded for days on a lonely storm-swept lighthouse. (I think the man involved was Edward Ward.)

Shortly after his harrowing adventure, I wrote this sketch for the Queen's Coronation Music Hall. Jon Pertwee and I played the Keepers and Arthur Askey made a brief appearance. It went very well and since then this piece has been played in many countries by top performers such as Jimmy Edwards, Tony Hancock, Dave King, Robert Dhery (who later expanded the idea into a complete show, 'Vos Geules les muettes') and by numerous others as well, without my permission.

THE LIGHTHOUSE KEEPERS

As it is full of props and hokum the sketch works in most languages, in fact you could probably play it in a nonsense language just as easily. Playing it, you also get very wet.

This sketch is usually set up by a 'front cloth' or on-camera announcement.

ANNOUNCER: The treacherous coasts of   have claimed many tall ships – and brave men. Constantly on watch against these disasters are the coastal guardians of our shores, the lighthouse keepers of   . When the great storms blow and the tempest rages, these gallant men are often cut off from the mainland for weeks on end.

(A stab of dramatic music and storm sound effects cover the transition to the lighthouse set. This is half of a circular room with a low-arched doorway set to stage right, and a heavy iron-bound outer door, set to stage left, while a porthole is set dead centre. It opens and closes and can be seen through.

Steps lead off-stage in a winding spiral from the arched open doorway, and the walls are equipped with a large old-fashioned barometer and a small curtained alcove. A table and two chairs are the only furnishings. As the storm reaches its height, with a terrific lightning flash and a deafening clap of thunder, the two keepers stumble down the stairs. The first one carries a storm lantern and turns on the light in the small cabin. The second keeper is carrying a mermaid. Her lovely arms are round his bearded neck. Both the keepers are wearing shiny yellow oilskins and rubber thigh boots. On their 'fringe-bearded' heads they sport sou'westers. The second keeper (the older one – though both are apparently ancient) stands dead centre for a moment, hefting the pretty mermaid in his arms. He eyes her all over)

SECOND KEEPER: *(Ruminatively)* There must be a way.
FIRST KEEPER: *(Flinging open the outer heavy door)* Aye. Somehow.

(The Second Keeper crosses to the open door (which opens down-stage) as a wave apparently hits the lighthouse and water (warm) cascades over the Keepers and the mermaid)

SECOND KEEPER: *(Throwing her off-stage out through the door)* Goodbye, darlin'. We'll try again on Saturday. *(Terrific splash)*
FIRST KEEPER: *(Shouting 'off')* And bring your sister!

(I should explain that the small cabin is really one half of a low-sided waterproof 'tank', made up of the set itself and a battened plastic tarpaulin, which is supported down-stage by a six-inch-high plank, round which its end is wrapped. This contains most of the water which enters the set. The Keepers return to centre-stage, after closing the heavy outer door with a clang.

FIRST KEEPER: Aye, Angus.

(We've played this sketch with just about every accent known, from Mummerset through French, Italian, German and Polish to rich Pakistani. For this version we'll use Scottish)

FIRST KEEPER: Forty days and nights yon terrible storm has been blowing – forty terrible lonely days and nights without relief. *(He turns dramatically towards the inner archway stairs, down which the light is shining)* Forty days and nights keeping the old light burning. God bless the old light! *(Both Keepers remove their sou'westers and clutch them over their hearts)* Well, Angus, it's time to do our duty. We must make up the log.
ANGUS: Aye, aye, Hamish. Time for the log. *(He sits behind the table and opens a heavy book, sucking his pencil preparatory to writing)*
HAMISH: January 26th! Fortieth day of the great storm. *(Angus writes laboriously)* The St Levi's light has now been cut off from the mainland by heavy seas for five continuous weeks. *(Pauses)* State of the tide? Ah! *(Turns to Angus)* Is it high tide or low tide, Angus?
ANGUS: I'll just check. *(He goes over to the central porthole and opens it. It opens down-stage and he promptly gets hit by a large bucketful of water and prop fish. Note: we used real fish on television – not to be recommended)*

136

ANGUS: *(A pause, then he turns to Hamish)* It's high tide.

HAMISH: State of the barometer? Check it, Angus!

(Angus goes over to the old-fashioned barometer and gives it a light tap. It falls off the wall)

HAMISH: Och! The glass has fallen.

(Angus enters the fact into the log)

HAMISH: *(Dramatically)* Forty days and nights without relief. We'd have starved to death, cut off from the relief ship, our stores gone, if it hadn't been for the old oil tanker that crashed upon the rocks below. *(Takes off his hat)* God bless the old oil tanker and her gallant crew.

(Angus fills his mug from a battered coffee pot, offering another mug to Hamish)

ANGUS: Another cup of petrol, Hamish?

HAMISH: Nay, laddie, I've had enough for one day. *(Continues)* 'Tis a terrible storm out there, Angus. But our duty is clear: we must keep the old light burning. *(They both stand up)* Forty days and nights without relief. Still no sign of the relief ship but we must carry on *(Hats off)* keeping the old light burnin'.

(Hamish turns towards the open archway with its light streaming down intermittently as the great lantern beams sweep round high above them)

HAMISH: *(Poetically, with full oratory)* Shine on, o great light! Shine on! Your pure white finger of light sweeping out across the tormented seas, guidin' the storm-tossed sailor home to a safe harbour! Shine on, great light, shine on!

(There is a heavy click and the light goes out)

HAMISH: Och, hell! The old bitch has gone out again. Do your duty, Angus.

ANGUS: Aye, aye, Hamish. *(He draws aside the curtain covering the small alcove and we see a gas-meter hidden there. Angus puts a coin into the meter and turns the dial switch. The coin drops down into the coin-box beneath and the great searchlight immediately comes on. Angus then removes the coin-box and retrieves his coin)*

HAMISH: Back to the log. *(As soon as Angus is seated and ready to write)* Is the wind from the east or from the west?

ANGUS: *(Wearily goes over to the porthole and opens it to receive the full blast of the large bucketful of water and prop fish. Angus licks his finger and holds it up to test the wind direction)*

ANGUS: From the west!

(During their dialogue, the foghorn above them has boomed out – this being timed to coincide with the pauses in their lines. Suddenly it stops)

HAMISH: Angus, did ye no hear somethin'?

ANGUS: What should I no hear, Hamish?

HAMISH: Did ye no hear that the foghorn didna' sound? So you'd no hear it.

ANGUS: Aye. You're richt. I *no* heard the foghorn.

HAMISH: Then do your duty, Angus!

(Angus reluctantly goes over to the porthole and looks at the audience – or into camera – as he breathes in. Then he flings open the porthole and gives a 'foghorn' shout, a cross between a bellow and a giant hiccup – the water and fish hitting him full on his wide-open mouth as he cups his hands round it for the foghorn effect. He staggers back into the cabin)

HAMISH: Dinna' worry, Angus. I'll go and fix it.

(Hamish swings into action and we hear his running footsteps racing round and round the lighthouse tower as he races up the stairs. There is a short pause, the foghorn blasts out again on high and we hear the running footsteps returning rapidly down the stairs. Hamish re-appears running down the last few steps and into the cabin, which he can't stop circling until Angus restrains him. Suddenly Angus sees something. He points and a red flare is seen outside the porthole)

ANGUS: A red flare, Hamish! There, on the horizon – a red flare!

HAMISH: Dear God, it can't be! The relief ship on the horizon! *(He rushes over to the porthole and flings it open. Angus expects Hamish to be covered in water and fish, but nothing happens. On the horizon we see a small model ship, with all its lights burning and smoke coming out of its funnel)*

HAMISH: *(Pointing at it)* It *looks* like the relief ship.

ANGUS: Are ye sure, Hamish?

HAMISH: I'll make certain, Angus. *(He reaches out through the porthole, picks up the model ship and brings it inside)*

HAMISH: *(Calling to the little ship)* Are you the relief ship?

TINY VOICE: No, we're not.

HAMISH: Sorry to trouble you.

TINY VOICE: Not at all!

(Hamish puts the ship back on the horizon and it steams away with a distant funnel-blast)

ANGUS: *(Thoughtfully)* Hamish?

HAMISH: Aye, Angus.

ANGUS: Did ye no think yon ship was a wee bit small?

HAMISH: Aye, Angus, but then you must remember that it was a long way away – on the horizon.

ANGUS: *(Considering this with a shrug of his shoulders)* Aye, you're right. My God, what's that?

A thunderous clanging is heard as someone knocks on the great metal outer door. Hamish and Angus huddle together in terror as the door creaks open. There is a short pause and a frogman in a milkman's cap and apron (but otherwise full scuba gear) enters, his flippers slapping the floor. He carries a wire cage of milk bottles)

MILK DIVER: *(Taking his snorkel out of his mouth)* One pint or two?

(Hamish and Angus have relaxed now they know their visitor is not the phantom of the Flying Dutchman)

HAMISH: *Two.* It's Saturday.

MILK DIVER: Ta ta, mate. See you Monday. *(He exits in a storm of water, as fish and a large rubber octopus are thrown in)*

ANGUS: You've got to hand it to the United Dairies.

(A loud siren is heard and a funnel blast. A red flare shines in through the porthole)

ANGUS: 'Tis the relief. My God, Hamish, it really is the relief! They're here!

HAMISH: *(Solemnly, taking his hat off and clutching it yet again)* Aye, Angus. You're right. 'Tis the relief! Our prayers are answered. Hurray, hurray!

(They clutch each other and dance round in a joyous embrace. A knock is heard on the outer door and Angus and Hamish grab each other in anticipation)

ANGUS/HAMISH: Come in! Come in!

(The door swings open and in come two pretty girls, dressed in bikinis and sou'westers, wellington boots and transparent plastic oilskins. They look very sexy. Angus and Hamish react.

ANGUS: I'll say one thing for the service, Hamish. When they send relief – they send *relief*!

HAMISH: Aye, Angus. Now, there's only one thing left to do.

ANGUS: What's that, Hamish?

HAMISH: *(Joyfully)* Put that bloody light out!

(Black-out as the two old keepers chase the screaming girls round the lighthouse)

Many years ago I got in very hot water for doing this sketch on television. Let me make it clear that with one English grandfather and three British uncles having been 'Through the Chair' in Freemasonry, the only thing that has stopped me humbly requesting admission to the craft has been my very Catholic South American family, who would probably drop dead if I became one of the Brethren.

My respect and admiration for what I have learned of the craft is unbounded. Therefore I ask the Brethren to think kindly of this harmless piece of nonsense.

THE GREAT GUILD

A huge bathroom with black and white linoleum tiles on the floor. The echoing walls are white-tiled and a large old-fashioned bath stands on its cast-iron lion feet in one corner, opposite a big window.

Seated on an impressive nineteenth-century wooden toilet commode is the Grand Master of the Great Guild of British Bath Craftsmen. Beside him stands a Master Tyler. They are both dressed in the traditional garb of bowler hats and bare chests, with celluloid collars and black knitted ties, and around their waists they are wearing large white bath towels with the letters BBC (standing for British Bath Craftsmen) on them. Their feet are shod in gartered dark wool socks and large black boots. (If this is done as a radio sketch, the scene is set with echoing bathroom sounds)

VOICE-OF-DOOM COMMENTATOR: In the great inner sanctum sanctorum of the Guild of British Bath Craftsmen sits the Grand Master Plughole Borer on the throne of meditation and beside him stands the Master Tyler with his long scroll of records printed on double-soft tissue. The atmosphere is tense as the ceremony of the initiation of an apprentice bidet-installer is about to begin.

(Three knocks are given by the Master Tyler, using a long-handled sink plunger)

VOICE-OF-DOOM COMMENTATOR: The Master Tyler gives the three knocks with the mighty inverted sink plunger of his office. This is the signal that the initiation ceremony is about to commence.

(Three knocks are heard coming from outside the great bathroom)

GRAND MASTER: Who knocketh upon the great door?

VOICE OUTSIDE: One who would gain admittance to the great bathroom.

MASTER TYLER: Has he the coin of admittance?

VOICE OUTSIDE: He has.

MASTER TYLER: Then place the coin of admittance into the slot of acceptance.

(Sound of coin being inserted into the coin-box on the convenience door)

VOICE OUTSIDE: This he has done.

MASTER TYLER: Now turn the handle – till the mystic word 'vacant' is no longer visible.

(The handle is turned)

VOICE OUTSIDE: This too he has done.

MASTER TYLER: Enter the great bathroom and stand upon the first square of the sacred linoleum.

(The door opens and three pairs of feet march in. The door is shut and the bolt rattles home)

GRAND MASTER: Does the mystic sign now read 'Engaged'?

VOICE OF ACCOMPANYING BATHROOM GUARD: It does.

VOICE-OF-DOOM COMMENTATOR: *(Reverently)* The Initiate, whose head is bared and who wears the short towel of the apprentice, is flanked on either side by the two bathroom guards – one wearing the silver chain and plug and the other bearing the ancient ceremonial black ball-cock. Both wear bowler hats and are girt round their loins with spotless white towels, with the letters BBC – British Bath Craftsmen.

GRAND MASTER: The Initiate now stands on the first squares of the great linoleum-tiled floor. Does he wish to advance?

INITIATE: I do. *(His voice is trembling with respect and fear)*

GRAND MASTER: Then advance, oh child of ignorance, to the light of knowledge.

(The three of them – Initiate and guards – step forward in unison, their heavy boots clunking down on the echoing linoleum floor)

GUARD: One, two, three, one, one/two!

(As their short steps forward are completed, the Master Tyler bangs down his inverted gavel/sink plunger three more times)

GRAND TYLER: Are you ready to answer the questions of initiation, oh novitiate?

APPRENTICE: I am.

GRAND MASTER: Answer without fear, oh apprentice novitiate! Wilt thou then?

APPRENTICE: I will.

ALL: So must it be. *(The echoing words resound in the great chamber)*

MASTER TYLER: Hast thou on at least three occasions forgotten thy tools?

APPRENTICE: *(Proudly)* I have.

MASTER TYLER AND GUARDS: He has.

MASTER TYLER: Hast thou bored the straight and true plug hole and inserted thereinto and withdrawn therefrom the non-fitting plug?

APPRENTICE: I have.

143

ALL: He has.

MASTER TYLER: And, finally, the great question. Hast thou ever left any bathroom in the state in which the owner would wish to find it?

APPRENTICE: *(Triumphantly)* I have never!

ALL: He has not. *(Pause)* Never!

APPRENTICE: All these things I have done, thereby upholding the finest traditions of the great craft of plumbing.

ALL: That he has.

GRAND MASTER: Then place in his right hand the sink plunger of Truth and in his left hand the ball-cock of Release! Round the Initiate's neck hang the chain of office, from which dangles the plug handle of propriety.

(The guards do so)

MASTER TYLER: Advance to the Seventh Square of the great chequerboard!

(They do so in perfect time and cadence – their heavy boots beating out the rhythm of the steps)

ALL: One, two, three, one, one/two!

GRAND MASTER: Are you now ready to take the oath, oh valiant apprentice novitiate?

APPRENTICE: I am. *(His voice is resolute with determination)*

GUARDS: He is.

MASTER TYLER: Do you solemnly swear to wait at least three days before answering a client's plea for help during the great freeze-up?

APPRENTICE: I do.

MASTER TYLER: Do you acknowledge the rules and regulations of the Great Guild of Master Plumbers, Plug-hole Borers and Bidet Fixers?

APPRENTICE: I do.

MASTER TYLER: And, finally, do you swear by Thomas Crapper, the great plumber in the sky, never to send in a bill for less than *three* times the just amount?

APPRENTICE: *(With total commitment)* I do.

ALL: He does! *(A great shout of 'Hallelujah' and a few bars of the 'Hallelujah Chorus' rise to the echoing low ceiling)*

GRAND MASTER: Well done, thou true and faithful apprentice.

ALL: Bloody good show, mate.

GRAND MASTER: Now, oh apprentice, you have passed the test and been put to the great question. Are you now ready to face the ordeal?

APPRENTICE: *(With quavering courage)* I am.

ALL: He is. He will. He must!

GRAND MASTER: Bend over the Great Bath of Ritual Cleansing!

ALL: He has.

GRAND MASTER: Light the blow torch of knowledge!

(The blow torch is lit)

GRAND MASTER: Apply the great torch to that seat of reason, where the apprentice plumber keeps his brains. *(The torch is applied to the apprentice's backside)*

APPRENTICE: Gawd! *(He leaps into the ritual bath with a loud splash. Hissing steam rises)*

GRAND MASTER: Crack the ritual bottle of sweet sparkling Australian sherry over the apprentice's head!

(The guard does so with a splintering crash)

APPRENTICE: Cor blimey!

GRAND MASTER: Launch the new apprentice, in his sacred bath of ritual cleansing, down the slipway of life and out into the world, through the great bathroom window.

(To a rousing chorus of 'Land of Hope and Glory' the bath rumbles out through the crashing glass and crumbling frame of the window to splash down far below in the mighty Thames River, the apprentice giving a wailing scream as it does so)

GRAND MASTER: The ceremony is over, gentlemen. Please adjust your ceremonial dress before leaving.

Of all the useless crafts in the world, firework making seems to me to take pride of place. Regularly, in celebration of the thwarting of Guy Fawkes in his attempt to blow up the British Houses of Parliament, many innocent men, women and children gravely injure or even kill themselves with British fireworks.

Recently there has been an outcry against this nonsense but it hasn't stopped the sale of these potentially lethal devices – which I must admit I thoroughly enjoyed as a child and then later as an adult with my own children.

Handel even wrote music to accompany the Royal Fireworks, and recently, to celebrate the Royal Wedding of HRH Prince Charles to Lady Diana Spencer, yet another magnificent display of Royal Fireworks got a little out of control.

This is a tribute to the great artificers of this murderous method of public enjoyment, who manufacture their noisy and colourful products under the same safety precautions as any other arsenal of democracy.

THE FIREWORK MAKERS

The Boardroom of the Whizzo Fireworks Company. At the long conference table are seated a number of middle-aged men and one very ancient member of the Board. Chairing the meeting is the Managing Director, Sir Arthur Crackle, a pompous, self-important but very worried man. Behind his chair is a large picture window, through which we can see the firework factory area, consisting of seven single-storey huts surrounded by blast-walls. They are numbered one to seven in large numerals and are, in fact, practical models, such as one would use in a giant diorama. These give a three-dimensional perspective to the scene. (For the radio version of this piece the Chairman sets the scene)

SIR ARTHUR: Gentlemen, the Whizzo Fireworks Company faces a crisis unparalleled in our long history. Sales of Whizzo fireworks and pyrotechnics have over the last financial year hit a new low. Inconceivable as it may seem, the British public seems to have lost its traditional compulsive interest in pyrotechnic displays.

BOARD: *(Together)* Shame! Impossible! Don't you believe it! It can't be! *Not* the British! Never!

SIR ARTHUR: I, too, could scarcely credit the evidence of my own eyes, but when you see the final figures on the sales chart you will realize that things have come to a pretty pass. Here they are. See for yourselves!

BOARD: Good God! Look at that! Right off the scale! Disaster! Bankruptcy staring us in the – the – the – er . . .

SIR ARTHUR: Face. Precisely! Out there *(He turns to the window)* our employees are hard at work turning out everything from Mafeking Rousers to Bangkok Air Raids. But still our sales figures slump disastrously.

BOARD: Why? What reason can there be? What's oop, Sir Charles? What's bloody happening? What's oop?

SIR ARTHUR: Costs. That's what's oop. Inflation, in all its grisly horror. High wages, the cost of raw materials, VAT. That's what's bloody oop! Do you realize, gentlemen, that the ha'penny banger of yesteryear, that gave such simple pleasure to millions by tying them to cats' tails, now costs 10p? I tell you, gentlemen, today only the most dedicated vandal will sacrifice 10p of his beer-money for the innocent joys of letting off a banger inside an old lady's shopping bag.

BOARD: Shame! Socialism – that's what did it. Bloody do-gooders. Shoot the lot of 'em! Blow 'em up!

SIR ARTHUR: We've tried everything. Our new Roman Candle – Nero's Orgy – which sold at the very reasonable figure of 50p and gave a noble display of *(He makes the noises, which are actually authentic but filtered through the audio synthesizer so that they are almost human in quality)* Phizz! Whizz! Whoosh! Bang! Crash! Crackle! Pop! Zooiee! *(Rapidly)* Bang-bang-bang! Orange balls. Wheeee! Pop! Bright red ones! Bang! Whoosh! Brilliant yellow stars! And crackle-crackle-crackle! Shooooosh! Golden rain! A marvellous 50p's worth. And look what happened!

BOARD: Well?

SIR ARTHUR: Nothing! A big fat zero. We had the lot returned. Had to flog 'em to Iran for crowd control. Disaster.

OLD IDIOT: What about the old-fashioned fireworks? I've got a little something . . . *(He's so old he can barely speak)* . . . here – an old favourite of my dear wife's, God rest her soul . . . *(Pause)* whoever she was. It goes fizz – whooie – putt, putt, putt, poop, poop, wheeeei – crackle, crackle – foh! And it only costs 25p.

VOICE FROM BOARD: Yes, what about the traditional fireworks?

Catherine-wheels and Jumping Crackers and those aeroplane things that go fizz, wheeeeeeeeeee, putt-putt, whizzzz, plop! What about them?

SIR ARTHUR: Can't give 'em away. Trouble is – television.

BOARD: Television? What's that got to do with fireworks? Explain yourself, sir.

SIR ARTHUR: Aye, television. That's the nigg . . . I mean the black gentleman in the wood pile. Too much violence, you see. The public are *satiated* with it. It's put paid to the 'pretty ones' forever. Forget the Flower Pots and Volcanoes, the Celestial Cascades and all those lovely fizz – whoosh – crackle – crackle, whee – pop – pop – pop multi-coloured stars and fairy lights. Gone! Gone for ever. Your average schoolboy and teenage layabout wants a full-blooded bang, crash, smash, zowieee, boom, boom, in blinding, bloody, lethal, sunbright orange with a two-hundred-foot-high filthy black mushroom cloud for his 50p. That's what bloody television's done. Spoiled the kids. What with Vietnam, Iran and Northern bloody Ireland! The kids want the real thing.

BOARD: Then give it to 'em.

SIR ARTHUR: Can't. Vickers Armstrong wouldn't like it. We'd be moving in on the arms racket. Aye! Now *if* we could produce a small plastic hand grenade, which still squeezed past the authorities and could just about pass for a firework, we'd have it made. But *cost* – there's the rub. Cost!

BOARD: Aye, cost. What's to do then?

SIR ARTHUR: I'll tell you, gentlemen. Out there at this moment in shed number one is our top pyrotechnician Grace Abercrombie . . .

BOARD: Good old Grace! Our Gracie! Right raver, our Gracie!

SIR ARTHUR: Yes! *Our* Gracie is on double overtime – busting a gut – working her little arse off to produce our new secret weapon.

BOARD: *(Gasps)* What is it, Sir Arthur?

SIR ARTHUR: A revolutionary new firework made out of explosive marzipan and cheap radioactive waste. We are going to call it the Great Bombay Disaster – Grace has designed it to do fizz – crackle – boooom! Baang! Karooom! Wheeeeee! Craaash! Ooooing! *(Terrific echo)* Rumble! Kerrash! Tinkle-tinkle. In scarlet and deep sickening purple and – this is the best part, gentlemen – it will only cost – wait for it – 4p. Four pence!

BOARD: *(Amazed)* Four pence? Really? Incredible! Genius! Well done, Sir Arthur!

SIR ARTHUR: Aye! *(Reverently)* That girl's a bloody genius. *(Pause)* Nice tits, too. Just think of it!

BOARD: Aaah! Beautifully built! What knockers! Like policemen's helmets!

SIR ARTHUR: No, the cost. The price. Gracie's going to give the British public what it wants – for *four* pence.

OLD IDIOT: I thought she charged more.

SIR ARTHUR: The firework, Lord Fondling! The Great Bombay Disaster. It will only cost four pence! What a historic moment this is! Out there in sheds one to seven our eager staff are waiting for the result, which could save Whizzo Fireworks and two hundred jobs. It's all up to you, Gracie, my girl. Let go the fourpenny Disaster!

(The phone bell rings. Sir Arthur picks up the receiver)

SIR ARTHUR: Right, Gracie! The Board's delighted. Let 'er rip, girl!

BOARD: Good luck, Gracie! Well done, love!

OLD IDIOT: Remember Brighton, dear!

SIR ARTHUR: *(Slamming down receiver)* Now we shall see some real fireworks!

(There is a distant fizz – then an almighty whoosh! Baang! Craash! Kerzoom! and a colossal explosion)

SIR ARTHUR: *(Stunned)* Oh Gawd! There goes shed number one, two, three, four, five, six and bloody seven!

(The Boardroom ceiling collapses and the big picture window blows in. As the dust and debris settle, the old idiot pipes up in a quavering tone of delighted awe)

OLD IDIOT: Just imagine! All that for four pence!

The art of television interviewing is an elusive one and even the most successful 'confronters' can get into trouble. Videotape has obviated the danger of losing a hard-won reputation at a stroke, but occasionally television interviewers get over-confident and for the sake of a gimmick will 'do it' live.

I remember with joy watching Erich Von Stroheim being confronted by a very confident BBC anchorman, way back before videotape and at a time when 'Auntie Beeb' was still playing it by the Reithian rules of Calvinistic conservatism. Stroheim, with his Prussian arrogance and shining, shaven bullet-head, demolished the unlucky interviewer by answering the question: 'Did you enjoy Hollywood?' with: 'Hollywood treated me like a well-kept whore.' The flummoxed BBC spokesman faintly replied: 'How jolly.' In the event, it was probably the only thing there was to say.

Over the years I have seen some near-disasters on live TV, my favourite being when that splendid actor Robert Donat played Thomas à Becket in *Murder in the Cathedral*. Having been mis-cued a number of times during the dress rehearsal by an inexperienced studio floor manager, Donat was apprehensive about the transmission.

Just before his cue, the young assistant once again gave Donat a premature signal. He reacted by giving the youngster the two-fingered 'up yours!' sign. As he did so, the red light opposite him came on, indicating that he was on the air. Immediately Donat switched the extended fingers round into the gesture of a pontifical blessing and continued the scene with the words: 'Blessed are the peacemakers!'

Well fielded, sir!

After watching artists and anchormen struggling against television's Murphy's Law, I wrote this sketch.

CONFRONTATION – LIVE FROM TIBET

A monastery high up on the icy plateaux of the Tibetan mountains. Four saffron-robed Lamas with impressive headgear and holding strange instruments stand behind a wizened Chief Lama of great age and venerable appearance. Only the sound of the keening wind breaks the silence, until the camera widens its horizon, to reveal the reverent figure of the American commentator, Clyde Quigley.

CLYDE: And here, live from Tibet via satellite, I am in the august presence of that great religious leader and mystical Tibetan Titan U-Tug. *(His tone of voice is that used by commentators when speaking inside cathedrals and concert halls – a mixture of stage-whisper and muted vibrant power. Clyde moves lithely towards the silent group of Tibetan mystics, still commentating in sepulchrally muted tones)* As I approach this great Tibetan guru – backed by his faithful acolytes – I feel a great sense of prideful awe when I realize that it was *I*, Clyde Quigley, who was chosen to conduct the U-Tug interview – a Tibetan first! This is a confrontation between the timeless wisdom of the East and the technology of the West! A meeting of giants.

(Clyde feels he might have gone a little bit too far on that last statement but only modifies it slightly)

CLYDE: By that, of course, I mean the giant magical intellects of U-Tug and myself, the simple respectful representative of a giant corporation – the National Broadcasting Corporation of America.

(By this time, Clyde has reached the saffron-robed group and is about to pop the questions)

CLYDE: For me personally this is a great moment. *(He turns to confront U-Tug – his voice now taking on the hard-edged incisive quality of the true 'Trial by Television' interviewer)* Your Holiness, U-Tug, in greeting you with all the good wishes and respect of the people of our great nation . . . *(Before he can get into the question-and-answer bit, U-Tug interrupts him with an imperative gesture of his long-fingered hands)*
U-TUG: We welcome the stranger. *(His voice is ancient but clear)*

(The four monks behind their great leader echo his words in chorus)

MONKS: Welcome the stranger.
CLYDE: *(Proudly)* And we return that gracious greeting. Now, Your Holiness . . .
U-TUG: *(Foiling him once again with hand raised and speaking in a piping voice)* It is destiny, stranger!
CLYDE: Naturally! A great moment in the history of both our peoples. Now . . .
U-TUG: *(Stopping him in full flight)* We welcome the stranger in our traditional manner – with the sound of the Fo!

(The first monk produces a Fo – a cross between bicycle handlebars and a French horn. It is made of something traditional like yak horn)

FIRST MONK: The sound of the Fo! *(He blows it and it makes a loud Fo sound)*

CLYDE: Most impressive! Quite charming! Now, Your Holiness . . .

U-TUG: *(Stopping him again)* We also welcome the stranger with the sound of the Ho-Ho.

MONKS: The sound of the Ho-Ho.

(The second monk raises his Ho-Ho – a bifurcated tube of considerable size which, when blown, makes a Ho-Ho sound, like two giant ducks breaking wind)

CLYDE: Enchanting! Quite delightful!

U-TUG: *(Warming to his task of Welcoming the Stranger properly)* We also welcome the stranger with the sound of the Umpah-Umpah.

MONKS: The sound of the Umpah-Umpah.

(The third monk blows into his Umpah-Umpah, which is coiled round him like a

great snake, ending in a bell-shaped orifice which gives the sound a singularly rude quality. The noise by this time is becoming deafening and Clyde has to raise his voice to get over the rhythmical cacophony of it all)

CLYDE: I feel honoured at such a reception. But there are vital questions to be asked and answered. For example, why . . .?

U-TUG: *(Arresting Clyde's first question)* And, lastly, we welcome the stranger with the sound of the great Sangammon.

(The last monk in line reaches up and grasps a bell rope which hangs above him. He pulls on it. An enormous bell of great power and disharmonic resonance sounds above him. It is completely deafening. As the bell sounds, the monk goes up with the rope and continues ascending and descending, accompanied by the sounds of the Fo, the Ho-Ho and the Umpah-Umpah)

CLYDE: *(Desperately)* U-Tug, great master of the Oriental world. Why? How? When? . . . *(His voice is drowned out and he grasps his throat, gasping and coughing with the dust descending from the great Sangammon above)*

U-TUG: *(Signalling the racket to stop, which it does in mid-Fo, Ho-Ho, Umpah-Umpah and Sangammon)* There! There! O stranger. You'll have to try again when we know you better.

MONKS: Know you better!

(They recommence their welcoming ritual with redoubled enthusiasm – leaving Clyde gasping for breath, with dust on the head and egg on the face)

When I was a boy the parks of London provided a safe green wonderland out of the roar of the capital's traffic, but it is a sad commentary on our times that these lovely landscaped refuges become a dangerous jungle once night falls.

Lovers strolling along the asphalt paths or lying close in the short grass can find their happiness only during the hours of daylight. By night it would be suicide. St James's Park, alone of all the great 'lungs of London', seems to be safe – but the presence of police and the nearby soldiers guarding the Palace may have something to do with it.

Why do we allow our beautiful parks to fall into the hands of the thug and the pervert? What has gone wrong? With these thoughts in my mind I came up with the following – a memory of something I saw during a lunchtime stroll (I couldn't afford lunch) through St James's Park many years ago.

LUNCHTIME IN THE PARK

The bridge over the lake in St James's Park. Ducks glide, quacking, in watery circles around the bridge, raising expectant beaks for the lunchtime crumbs. (This has always been a favourite spot for people to come and feed the ducks and the exotic water birds that find sanctuary on the lake. Only since the war have people brought their sandwiches as well. Before the war such al fresco meals were infra-dig)

A typical junior civil servant in a worn trilby hat and raincoat is furtively munching a sandwich from his battered briefcase. An Arab, in burnous and galabieh, strolls up and stands beside him, a carrier bag in his hand. As they feed the ducks with breadcrumbs an invisible bond is made. Something breaks through the cautious barriers of race. Finally the Arab breaks the silence.

ARAB: Lovely day.

CIVIL SERVANT: *(Nervously)* Yes, it is. Quite nice.

ARAB: What an oasis! It reminds me of the great oasis of Suleiman the Magnificent. No date palms there, either.

CIVIL SERVANT: Oh, quite so! No. There are no date palms here, that is, that *I* know of in St James's Park. *(His voice is very precise and he has no sense of humour)*

ARAB: Do you come here often?

CIVIL SERVANT: Yes. Every day. Well, when I say every day, I mean every working day. I'm at the Ministry of Public Works.

ARAB: I am at the Embassy. We don't work in public, only in private.

CIVIL SERVANT: Oh, no. Quite so! Which Embassy is that?

ARAB: The United Bedouin Nomad Republics. I am in charge of the camels.

CIVIL SERVANT: Really! I'm the assistant file clerk for the Sewage Department.

ARAB: How romantic! Must be a very important job.

CIVIL SERVANT: Quite so! Yes. Do you have a lot of camels in your charge?

ARAB: In the desert – thousands upon thousands. As countless as the stars in the heavens. Here – none. *(He lowers his voice)* We get our best breeding stock from the London Zoo. A private arrangement.

CIVIL SERVANT: Really! *(He boldly extends his sandwich bag)* Would you care for a sandwich? These are tongue.

ARAB: How generous. However, we are forbidden to eat the tongue as it comes from the mouth of the beast. But we *are* allowed eggs.

CIVIL SERVANT: Oh, these are banana and pickle and these are cheese and dates.

ARAB: What a delightful choice! Most kind. Most kind. *(He munches at the small quarter-cut sandwich)* Delicious!

CIVIL SERVANT: Mum makes them.

ARAB: Mum? That is part of Harrods?

CIVIL SERVANT: No, *my* mum! My mother. She makes them. Wonderful cook, my mum!

ARAB: *(Reverently)* Wonderful lady. Wonderful sandwiches. I do her reverence. A good mother is a blessing from Allah.

CIVIL SERVANT: Oh, yes. Quite so! She's with the Ministry, too. She *does* for them.

ARAB: Does what for them? She dances? A nautch girl?

CIVIL SERVANT: No, she's a Maintenance Engineer.

ARAB: Builds the drains?

CIVIL SERVANT: No, she's a cleaner.

ARAB: Oh, she cleans the drains.

CIVIL SERVANT: *(Changing the subject)* Would you like another sandwich?

ARAB: *(Taking one)* You are too hospitable! You are part Arab, perhaps?

CIVIL SERVANT: Welsh. Part Welsh. On Grandad's side.

ARAB: *(Rummaging in his carrier)* Oh, really? Perhaps you would honour

156

me by accepting a small morsel of my tiffin. I regret I have no dates. Out of season.

CIVIL SERVANT: *(Taking the proffered morsel)* Oh, thank you. *(He cautiously eats it)* Quite nice, really. Sort of like a crunchy grape. What fruit is it? *(He swallows it)*

ARAB: Sheep's eyeball. Very nutritious. Difficult to get here. I was lucky with Fortnum & Mason's.

CIVIL SERVANT: *(Realizing the implication, but struggling to keep his cool and the sheep's eyeball down)* Oh, really? Very tasty! *(He hurriedly produces a small package)* Would you like a piece of my mum's cake?

ARAB: Delighted! *(Takes it)* What a lovely confection! Rich and dark. Full of Western promise. These dark things . . . *(Interestedly)* . . . they are flies? *(He munches away)*

CIVIL SERVANT: Oh, no, not in my mum's cake! No! Those are currants.

ARAB: Almost as tasty as flies! Most delicious! Please . . . *(He rummages once again in his Fortnum's carrier bag)* Ah! You'll love these chocolates.

CIVIL SERVANT: Oh! I love chocolate. *(Taking one)*

ARAB: No, no, take more than one! Here, have a handful! *(He pours a small pile of chocolate bits into the Civil Servant's palm)*

CIVIL SERVANT: *(Nervously taking one in his mouth)* They're very nice. I like the crunchy centre. *(He fills his mouth with the sweets and munches away)* Very nice. Nice and crunchy.

ARAB: *(Proudly)* They're a great delicacy. Chocolate-covered ants. The snack you can eat between feasts. Melts in your mouth – not in your hand!

(The full realization hits the Civil Servant, who chokes and hurriedly beats as polite a retreat as possible – heading precipitately for the nearest Gents)

CIVIL SERVANT: *(Gagging with his hand to his mouth)* Excuse me! Got to rush! I'm late. Nice to meet you. Thanks for – for – everything. Oops!

(He rushes off. The Arab stares after him meditatively, then turns back to the bridge rail)

ARAB: *(Shrugging his Bedouin shoulders)* Must have been his mother's cake! *(He concentrates on throwing bread to the ducks)* Here, duck, duck, duck, duck.

The mystique that surrounds unusual sports has an irresistible appeal for me and it has provided a theme for several of the pieces I conceived for radio and television. For instance, the joy of making *The Great British Nanny Race* in the early sixties must have communicated itself to millions of viewers, because many Nanny races have since raised money all over the country for various charities.

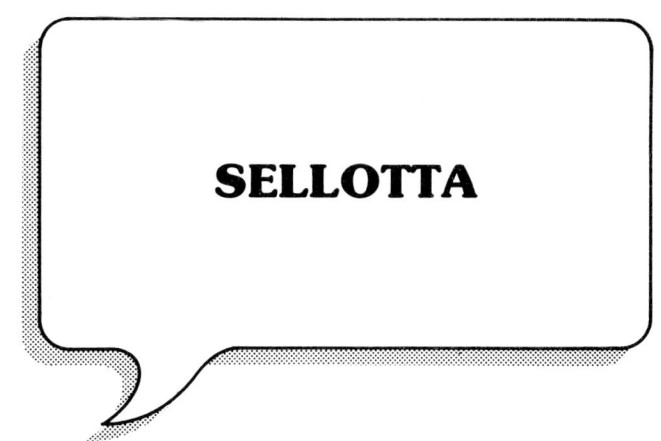

The race, as I saw it, in a brief flash of 'pottyvoyance', was a modern form of *Ben Hur* chariot-racing, using prams and an international gathering of ethnic 'nannies' as the ruthless competitors. The final result that we filmed en route from London to Brighton was a happy blend of slapstick and mayhem.

Even though we had a bunch of stuntmen, we still had to do a lot of the stunt-gags ourselves. We loved doing it and I still look back in wonder that we weren't all killed.

Since then I have filmed and recorded *Motor-Mowing Grand Prix*, which caught on in a big way and is now an established sport, *Drats*, which is played worldwide, *Boggling on Ice* and *Boggart Hunting*, with an invisible prey and anti-blood-sport saboteurs, and numerous other pre-Monty Python sporting gems.

Sellotta is of this genre of mystical sporting events – a weird ritualized sport akin to the mad Aztec game which was believed to have been played with a gutta-percha ball and probably included human sacrifice as well.

This piece was inspired by the immortal words of a *jaī-allaī* commentator who remarked: 'The ball is not visible to the spectators – one wonders how the players see it.' Or even if it exists at all!

The open side of a sellotta court, which is as long and as wide as space permits. The far wall is divided into squares and rectangles, with large numbers painted on them. The front wall, off which the players speed their ball, is also marked with symbols and numbers inside bold geometric patterns. The floor of the sellotta court is painted with lines and serving bases, and the whole impression conveyed by the playing pitch is one of the age-old tradition and sporting origins lost in the mists of antiquity.

For radio the commentator describes the scene.

COMMENTATOR: Here I am standing just outside the netted area of the Piddling Bassett sellotta court – the very first time that a sports commentary has been given during the course of this ancient and gruelling game. Beside me is Colonel Miles-Pastitt, the British authority on sellotta, which he describes as:

COLONEL: *(Very precise military voice)* The sport of princes.

COMMENTATOR: A great British sporting event!

COLONEL: Not exactly. British only by adoption from the ancient Peruvian sport of IncaToss, in which a live llama was believed to be used.

COMMENTATOR: Good heavens! How?

COLONEL: We don't actually know. We just believe it.

COMMENTATOR: The sellotta court is most impressive. Is it an exact copy of the ancient Peruvian one?

COLONEL: Not really, though parts of it are based on the meagre information that the Spanish Conquistadores have left us.

COMMENTATOR: Ah! Then it was also an ancient Spanish game as well?

COLONEL: No, and we can say that with some certainty. The Spanish only referred to the game. They never actually played it.

COMMENTATOR: I see. There are then actual extant Spanish references to this ancient Peruvian sport?

COLONEL: Not in writing, no. Sellotta is an oral tradition. You play it by ear. The only known reference to this sport by a living Spaniard was one made by Don Jose Garcia y Vega Butifarero, the well-known Hispanic sports historian and drunk. He was delirious at the time.

COMMENTATOR: Could you explain the layout of the sellotta court for us?

COLONEL: Certainly. The court or pitch, as we call it, is three times as long as it is wide and twice as wide as it is high. The plancha – or floor – is four times the height of the nearest player and is made entirely out of compressed llama droppings. This forms a compact and weather-resistant, if somewhat unpleasant, playing surface. It also nearly crippled us financially.

COMMENTATOR: Fascinating! What about the signs and symbols painted on the walls?

COLONEL: Yes. What about those? We try to wash them off but they keep coming back. Bloody perverts!

COMMENTATOR: Actually, I meant the large numerals and letters.

COLONEL: Ah, those, yes. Well, they are, as near as we can imagine them, the actual divisions and playing and scoring areas used by the Incas. In devising them, we had to attune ourselves to early Inca thinking.

COMMENTATOR: By research and scholarship?

COLONEL: No, by getting blind drunk. The Incas always got legless before playing sellotta. That way they could stand the pain.

COMMENTATOR: Was it intense?

COLONEL: No, it was in the open. The game is played *al fresco*, not in tents!

(Two voices are heard approaching)

FIRST VOICE: I'll take the upwind if you change at noon.

SECOND VOICE: All right, Humphrey. The moon is in its first quarter so the cross bias will compensate for the lack of solar wind.

COLONEL: Sellotta has highly mystical overtones – occult is probably the right word.

COMMENTATOR: Really?

COLONEL: No, just probably. Note the layout of the court markings: the large X on the facing wall, the huge Y on the side wall, and the giant P on the floor. Sellotta is a demanding game. It's all or nothing.

(The players take up their positions prior to commencing the ancient game)

FIRST VOICE: Mark.

SECOND VOICE: Yes, Humphrey?

FIRST VOICE: Rough or smooth? East or west?

SECOND VOICE: Up or down?

FIRST VOICE: Sideways.

SECOND VOICE: Your serve then.

(There is the sound of effort, a whizzing noise, a ricochet and more effort followed by the sound of skidding plimsolls and running feet, with speedy slaps and more high-speed ricochets. A crash of glass terminates the first rally. Applause from a crowd)

COLONEL: Nice rally! A little cautious at first but opening up beautifully after the third nozzle.

COMMENTATOR: Nozzle?

COLONEL: A technical term. Probably wrong.

JUDGE'S VOICE: *(On echo)* Advantage Buttersocks. Mackeson to serve. Bull Run – server to the goggle box! Upchat to marker!

COLONEL: A tense moment this. If Mark Mackeson can get his service into the chuckling lane he'll take the next two points.

161

COMMENTATOR: Could you explain that?

COLONEL: No time. There he goes!

(The server takes a short skidding run on the court. Great effort, a twang, ricochets, whizzing sounds and a splintering crunch. Crowd groan of disappointment)

COLONEL: Oh, bad luck! He mistled when he should have toed – probably the cross wind. Or it could have been his braces slipping.

COMMENTATOR: Their clothing is strangely colourful. Traditional almost?

COLONEL: Not really. Personal choice. Humphrey likes to play in Empire shorts and waders, with a gutta-percha bolero over a pink plastic petticoat, and Mark prefers a peppermint-striped nightshirt, with sequin appliqués, tucked into polythene jodhpurs and rope sandals. Every player dresses as he feels he should – until he is told to leave the court.

COMMENTATOR: By the umpire?

COLONEL: By the police. It's a very erotic game, sellotta. Last season was *un*believable. We were opened by the Lady Mayoress and closed by the Vice Squad. Yes, sellotta is growing in popularity every day. Ah, there goes the second rally!

(Another clearly heard and utterly incomprehensible rally takes place with a flurry of ricochets, skidding plimsolls and rope sandals finishing with a suction sound, like a great sink plunger being withdrawn from an enormous loo. The crowd is on its feet, frenzied with excitement)

COLONEL: Hear that? The crowd's gone mad. *(Shots are fired – screams and general mayhem)*

COMMENTATOR: Where *is* the crowd?

COLONEL: Miles away. It's far too dangerous a sport for spectators. God knows what would happen to them if we allowed them to watch.

COMMENTATOR: But the crowd sounds? I heard them.

COLONEL: A recording. Far safer. We record the crowd separately. Then we play the recording back after each rally.

COMMENTATOR: What are they watching, then?

COLONEL: Blue films. We find that gets them going. *Jane Goes Solo* is the best.

UMPIRE: *(On echo)* Third razzle in the second set. Advantage Mackeson. Buttersocks to thrust – match-point for game, set and soup.

COLONEL: By George! Things are heating up now. If Buttersocks makes this chukka, he'll be a dead certainty for the International Reuben-Sandwich Finals in Bogotá in 1999. Pity he'll be a bit old for it.

COMMENTATOR: Could you be more specific, Colonel?

COLONEL: *(Rudely)* Quiet man! It's a centre dribble! And there he goes!

(Skidding of plimsolls, effort and smashing ricochets, rebounding from everywhere, a final whizz and an almighty splash, glass breaks and an express train hits an elephant. 'Tarzan' yell and falling debris. The crowd goes berserk)

COLONEL: *(Mad with joy)* That I should live to see the day! What a *dribble* – a true four-by-two – and upwind at that. If only Obolensky was alive to see it! Well done, Humphrey!

(The two voices of the exhausted players approach)

FIRST VOICE: I tell you, Mark, I thought you'd get me on that first frazzle!

SECOND VOICE: Near thing, old man, near thing!

COMMENTATOR: Excuse me, but could I just see your bats?

HUMPHREY: Bats? *(Laughs)* Did you call them bats? Hear that, Mark? He called them *bats*.

MARK: *(Chuckling)* Easy to see you're no sellotta *aficionado*. These are our waffle boards – made out of high-impact asparagus. Bats, indeed! Cor!

COMMENTATOR: And the ball?

BOTH: Ah, *that's* quite different.

COLONEL: Yes. That is quite another kettle of fish.

COMMENTATOR: It's made out of fish?

(Gasp from both players)

HUMPHREY: You've got to be joking!

MARK: *(Seriously)* I say, old man, you're forgetting the game has religious overtones. Steady on!

HUMPHREY: Mystical! Sellotta is downright esoteric. We don't like rude remarks like that, you know.

COMMENTATOR: Could I see a sellotta ball?

COLONEL: Oh, all right, if you must! Show him one, Humphrey.

HUMPHREY: *(Reluctantly)* All right. Here! *(Rudely)* Seen enough?

COMMENTATOR: I didn't *quite* see it.

COLONEL: Show him again, Humphrey!

(In the television version, Humphrey opens and closes his hand very quickly)

HUMPHREY: There! *(Quickly)* Got it?

COMMENTATOR: I couldn't see it at all.

COLONEL: Nor you should. Sellotta is the fastest game on earth. No one can see the ball. Much too quick!

(A van draws up and two men crunch their way up to the conversing group)

COMMENTATOR: Who are these two chaps?

COLONEL: The ones in the white coats? Oh, they're marshals.

MARSHAL ONE: *(Reassuringly)* Now come along, lads. Time for tea – back you go!

HUMPHREY: No, shan't!

MARSHAL TWO: Now come along, lad! Crumpets for tea!

MARK: Oh, *(Reluctantly)* all right, but I won! Tell them *I* won, Humphrey!

HUMPHREY: Yes, he did, he did! That's a red motor bus you owe me, Colonel.

MARK: *(Bursting into tears)* I never get a red motor bus – only those bloody purple rubber crocodiles.

COLONEL: There, there! Lads, go along and have a nice tea and crumpets.

MARSHAL ONE: *(Whispering)* No need for the jackets, George. They'll come quietly.

MARSHAL TWO: Oh, sod it! I enjoy putting on the jackets – just my bloody luck!

(They go off muttering and chatting)

COMMENTATOR: Wait a minute. You mean to say . . . *(Realization dawns)* . . . that they're . . .? They're . . .?

COLONEL: Of course! How else could they play sellotta? It's all in the mind, you know, all in the mind.

COMMENTATOR: Then we can't see the ball – because there isn't one? *(He giggles hysterically)*

COLONEL: Precisely! Oh, by the way, the lads would like you to have this. *(He hands the Commentator a box clearly marked Sellotta Balls)*

COMMENTATOR: *(For radio)* What is it?

COLONEL: It's marked on the box. Sellotta Balls. Don't open it till I've gone. *(He walks away)* There's a good chap.

COMMENTATOR: *(Into mike)* I'm terribly sorry about that. They're a bit funny here. *(He chuckles)* I'll just open the box to see if there's a note inside. *(Box is opened)* No, nothing. I'll just make sure – turn it upside down. *(He does so and we hear the sound of about a dozen invisible sellotta balls bouncing about the place)*

COMMENTATOR: Oh, no! Not that! *Please* not that. Somebody – help me! Help! Heeeelp!

This one I dreamt up as a tribute to my dear old friend, the late Jack Warner. Many years before, my father (who was a remarkable psychometrist) 'picked up' that Jack, a close family friend, would become 'the best-known copper in Britain'. This was before Jack had appeared in the film *The Blue Lamp*, playing the part of the old 'bluebottle', P.C. Dixon.

DOXON OF DICK GREEN

When Ted Willis (now Lord Willis) decided to feature the defunct Dixon (he had been shot by Dirk Bogarde in the film) in a thirteen-part series for BBC Television, Pop told Jack that his prophecy would now start to come true. In fact *Dixon of Dock Green* ran for over twenty years and Jack died in his eighties – a much loved and certainly the *best-known* copper in Britain.

A musical feature of this long-running television series was the theme song, 'An Ordinary Copper', which was composed and played by Tommy Reilly on his harmonica, with words by Jack Warner. That harmonica theme became as familiar as did Jack's P.C. Dixon, with his cheery: 'Evening all!' at the start of the show. (Note: Jack Warner was the *British* entertainer and actor, *not* the Jack Warner of Warner Brothers in Hollywood!)

I'm happy to say that Jack loved the following gentle send-up of his 'Dixon of Dock Green' and wrote me a letter of thanks.

A quiet late evening in Dick Green, a London borough somewhere between Wapping and Ealing. A typical row of shops and premises, with apartments over the top of them, front the old High Street, which typifies P.C. Doxon's beat – his 'parish', as he calls it. Doxon, an ageing constable of many years' local experience in the borough, is the epitome of the old-time copper. He is also a bit deaf. A harmonica plays the theme music as Doxon approaches, his size fourteen boots ringing impressively on the pavement (and all through the action the harmonica music continues to play).

DOXON: Evening all! Well, things have been nice and quiet down here at the old Green since I last reported to you. (*The sound of his boots proceed slowly along the pavement*) Yers! Been a nice quiet week altogether. Sid Baker, that young tearaway, got engaged to Sally, the Salvation

Army lass, and seems to have given up the arson bit at last! Slasher Smith has been put away for doing up the vicar. Pleaded extenuating circumstances. Said the old boy gave him the come-on and he was using self-defence. *(Chuckles)* A likely story!

Then there's Margaret, our young telephonist, she got married to Sergeant Perkins, our sergeant, and about time, too! And – what else? Oh, yes! 'Fingers' Hoolahan, the local 'dip' – that's pickpocket – got caught with his hand in the till or rather in old Miss Watkins's skirt pocket. The old dear didn't want to press charges, and even offered him a home and thirty bob a week. Nice old girl!

'Allo! There's a light on in the old paint shop. *(Peers in)* No! Nothing to worry about. Just old Mrs O'Reilly in the back room. Probably stock taking. Funny old duck – I can 'ear 'er humming away there. Cor! What a card! *(Sound of old lady humming and singing 'Mother Macree')* Potters about at all hours, smoking that smelly old clay pipe of 'ers! Blimey, that old paint shop needs doing up – and a good clean out. *(His footsteps are past it now)* The whole place stinks of paraffin and kerosene. *(Mrs O'Reilly stops singing in mid-'Mother Macree', as a dull explosion and crackling flames tell us that the paint shop's gone)*

DOXON: *(Deaf as a board)* Yes! You don't 'arf meet some strange characters here at the Green. *(He stops and rattles a heavy door)* Take the bank here! Right next to the pawn shop. *(He chuckles – a rich copper's giggle)* Mr Montagu, the bank manager, has been there for twenty years. Never once has he spoken to old Solly Goldberg, the pawnbroker next door. And old Solly banks with him and all! Must be worth a fortune, old Solly. *(His footsteps renew their measured tread)* I'll bet he's got more money than old Mr Montagu. It's just plain snobbery. After all, they're both in the banking business.

(A car pulls up with a squeal of brakes. A door opens hurriedly and footsteps run across the pavement. Effort and a crash of glass, then a jumbled sound of objects being stuffed into a bag; back across the pavement go the footsteps, the car door slams and with a screech of tyres the car accelerates away, skids, then crashes into a lamppost – and bursts into flames)

DOXON: *(Oblivious)* Yers! Lovely night! Moon shining like a copper's bull's-eye lamp. Cor, you don't see the p'licemen with 'em nowadays, but when I started on the beat, the old bluebottles used to carry 'em. My grandad gave me 'is. I still use it even today. *(Another knowing chuckle)* What a character the old boy was! No juvenile delinquents in *his* day! He'd give 'em a good clip round the 'earhole and send 'em on their way. Marvellous man! Spent 'is life raising money for the borough's deaf children. There were a lot of 'em in them days. *(Chuckles again, as his feet stop pounding the beat)* 'Allo, 'allo, 'allo! The Thompsons are at it again.

(An argument between a young man and his wife can be heard inside a house)

DOXON: Funny how youngsters get so hot under the collar nowadays. In my day *(His feet continue their pavement pounding)* the wife kept her mouth shut. She knew that 'er husband had a hard day's work behind 'im and deserved a pint with 'is mates.

(The argument is getting more distant and very heated. Doxon is totally oblivious. The wrecked blazing car and the crackling flames of the paint shop have attracted

the attention of the fire brigade, who skid to a halt and start trying to put out a blaze that threatens the whole High Street)

DOXON: *(Pounding on)* I personally blame television. That's what's at the back of it all! Too much sex and violence!

(The Thompsons' row has now become violent, with breaking furniture and glass, and eventually Mr Thompson strangles Mrs Thompson amid blood-curdling yells)

DOXON: *(Happily bumbling on)* Still! Keep out of it, I always say. A copper's job is to keep the peace, not to act as a marriage counsellor. That's a job for the professionals – not that we're not professionals. Being a copper is no job for an amateur. *(For the first time he notices the harmonica music which is now very loud. P.C. Doxon has arrived at the end of the street where the harmonica player is standing)* 'Ere you, mate! You got a licence to play that thing?

HARMONICA PLAYER: *(Pausing in mid-suck-and-blow)* No, mate.

DOXON: *(Very officiously)* Right then! You'll come along with me.

HARMONICA PLAYER: On what charge?

DOXON: Playing a musical instrument without a street licence. Disturbing the peace.

HARMONICA PLAYER: 'Ere! Take your 'ands off of me!

DOXON: Resisting arrest!

(Sound of blow being struck)

DOXON: And striking a police officer in the pursuance of 'is duty!

(He blows his whistle. Sounds of police sirens. The fire-fighting is now sheer bedlam and utter chaos reigns)

DOXON: *(Fighting for his life)* See you all next week! Take care if you're driving. Cor! *(Uses his truncheon with splintering sounds)* Be kind to each other! And don't forget to look *both* ways when crossing the road!

(These useful tips are drowned out in the general mêlée)

Anyone who enjoyed the joyous pageantry of the Royal Wedding will wonder who was responsible for it. It was, of course, the result of the hard work and dedication of many people, but the buck stops at the top, in the office of the Lord Chamberlain.

During the course of some fascinating research into the processes by which visiting dignitaries are given an official greeting, royal birthdays celebrated, and State processions and banquets arranged, I met some extraordinary people who seem to live in another world – the dimension of Ruritania. The result was this sketch.

MASTER OF THE QUEEN'S REVELS

A large, dustily-curtained window gives a view of St James's Palace yard, where the guards are being changed in accordance with the age-old ritual. A door opens and a junior Palace official quietly enters while a quill pen is heard scratching.

JUNIOR OFFICIAL: *(Coughing discreetly)* Excuse me, Sir Bertrand. I hope I'm not disturbing you, sir?

SIR BERTRAND: *(An ancient official gnome)* No, my boy. I was just finishing the accounts for Her Majesty's Jubilee. That's the last payment to the contractors for the bunting and flagpoles.

JUNIOR: It must take quite a time to clear it all up, sir.

SIR BERTRAND: Indeed! This is for the jubilee of Her Majesty Queen Victoria. *(The pen continues to scratch, then is thrown down on to the desk)* Ah! That's finished! Now, then, young man, what can I do for you?

JUNIOR: It's about the Nawab of Gob, sir.

SIR BERTRAND: What about the Nawab of Gob?

JUNIOR: He's coming, sir. On the fifth of next month, and we don't seem to have made any special arrangements for his arrival.

SIR BERTRAND: Well, now, let's see. Is the Nawab of Gob important?

JUNIOR: He's the Divine Head of the State of Gob, by Supreme Right, the Appointed One, by His Celestial Father, the one and only true Gob, the Omnipotent Being, the All Highest . . .

SIR BERTRAND: Quite so, quite so! Does Gob produce anything?

JUNIOR: Dates, sir.

SIR BERTRAND: Anything else?

JUNIOR: Camels.

SIR BERTRAND: What else?

JUNIOR: Camel chips. The camels' droppings are rich in nitrates, sir.

SIR BERTRAND: Any oil?

JUNIOR: Not that I know of, sir, not in camel droppings.

SIR BERTRAND: *(Wearily)* I meant crude oil.

JUNIOR: Not as yet, sir, but they are drilling in the Gulf of Gob.

SIR BERTRAND: So! As yet! We can't really consider the Nawab of Gob as a royal guest of number one importance. Let's see . . . *(Rustle of papers)* Dates, fertilizer, camels. That's hard to assess in importance value as an honoured guest. I'll send for the expert. *(A desk phone key is depressed – a crackling voice answers)*

VOICE: *(On filter)* Yes, Sir Bertrand?

SIR BERTRAND: Send in Codpiece! We've got an official reception problem.

VOICE: Very good, sir.

SIR BERTRAND: You won't have met Codpiece yet. A first class fellah! Been here since the year dot. *(A timid knock on the door heralds Codpiece's arrival)*

SIR BERTRAND: Come in, Codpiece!

(The door opens and is gently closed, to admit Arthur Codpiece, an elderly, stooping clerk, whose dusty aura proclaims him to be a royal retainer of many years standing)

SIR BERTRAND: Morning, Codpiece.

CODPIECE: *(Whose precise voice is worn with age)* Sir Bertrand?

SIR BERTRAND: This is Marchmont. Old Harry Marchmont's boy.

CODPIECE: I had the honour of knowing your father, sir. I served under him for many years.

MARCHMONT: In the war, Mr Codpiece?

CODPIECE: In the royal cellars, sir. He was, as you know, sir, the royal wine taster for the great banquets. I understand that he has passed over, sir.

MARCHMONT: Yes. Cirrhosis of the liver. Very sudden!

CODPIECE: My sympathies. A great gentleman, sir.

SIR BERTRAND: *(Impatiently)* Yes, yes, very sad! Now, Codpiece, we have a problem. The Nawab of Gob. Know anything about him, Codpiece?

CODPIECE: His Serene Highness, the Nawab of Gob, is due to arrive at Portsmouth on the fifth of next month. Apart from that, Sir Bertrand, I know nothing. I was awaiting your orders, sir.

SIR BERTRAND: Well, now! What official reception shall we accord the Nawab?

CODPIECE: Ah, yes. We could welcome His Serene Highness the Nawab with a salute of twenty-one guns – provided, of course, that the Royal Navy has got a frigate available and that the Royal Dockyard is not on strike. The procedure would be that His Serene Highness is met by the frigate, which is dressed overall with flags of all nations – spelling out 'A Royal Welcome to His Serene Highness'. Then, the Admiral's barge will transport His Serene Highness on a tour of inspection of the mothball fleet, while the band of the Royal Marines plays selections from *HMS Pinafore*.

On his arrival at the quayside, His Serene Highness will be met by the Commandant of Number Two Commando and the city's civic dignitaries, who will grant him the keys to the City of Portsmouth. After a shore inspection of the Guard of Honour, His Serene Highness will be escorted to the Royal Daimler, then whisked to the railway station where the Royal Train will be waiting. A seven-course railway banquet will be served en route, with appropriate French champagne and other fine French wines and, on arrival at Victoria Station, His Serene Highness will be met by Her Majesty Queen Elizabeth. That is our Category A official welcome, Mr Marchmont.

SIR BERTRAND: Yes, quite so! But I don't feel that the Nawab of Gob quite rates that one. Not Category A.

CODPIECE: Then Category B, perhaps? In that case His Serene Highness the Nawab of Gob will be met on arrival at Portsmouth by a salute of ten guns from Her Majesty's minesweeper *Invincible* and escorted, in the Captain's barge, for a short inspection of the reserve mothball fleet of gunboats and fleet oilers. At the quayside, a small contingent of the Territorial Army and the Town Clerk will greet His Serene Highness. Then His Serene Highness will be awarded the key to the Town Hall, after which he will be driven, in the Ford Granada, to the railway station, where the royal coach will be provided, connected to the rear of the 9.14 to Victoria. During the journey a British Railways standard menu will be accompanied by Spanish champagne and South African wines, finishing off with a glass of Japanese Port. At Victoria, Her Majesty's representative, the Duke of Wobbling Baddeley, will greet His Serene Highness and take him to lunch at Simpsons in the Strand. Category B perhaps, Sir Bertrand?

SIR BERTRAND: *(Pausing thoughtfully)* Dates? Camel fertilizer? No, I don't think Category B.

CODPIECE: How about Category C, sir? On arrival at Portsmouth, a saluting gun from Her Majesty's dredger *Mudlark* will precede His Serene Highness's brief tour of inspection, in a liberty boat, round the fleet garbage-scow *Lady Macbeth*, followed by an official greeting by a platoon of the Chelsea Pensioners and the Town Beadle who will offer him the key to the executive washroom. His Serene Highness will then be driven in a Volkswagen to the station, where a reserved table in the buffet car will provide a box luncheon and a quarter bottle of Australian sweet sparkling sherry and a half carafe of Chilean plonk. At Victoria, His Serene Highness will be met by the representative of the Duke of Wobbling Baddeley, the Honourable Charles Knothole, and taken to the Golden Egg for a light brunch.

SIR BERTRAND: No, I don't think that quite fits the bill, either. What else have you got to offer us?

CODPIECE: Well, sir. There's only Category D left, sir. I'm reluctant to offer that one, sir.

SIR BERTRAND: *(Pompously)* Let me be the judge of that, Codpiece!

CODPIECE: *(Chastened)* Very well, Sir Bertrand. Category D it is. On arrival at Portsmouth, His Serene Highness the Nawab of Gob will be greeted by a fanfare of trumpets, using the mouthpiece only, and a quick blast on the funnel siren from Her Majesty's sanitary barge *Elsan*. A quick tour of the scrapyard by dinghy follows and, on the quayside, His Serene Highness will be greeted by two boyscouts and the Portsmouth borough dog-catcher. He will be offered the key to the local abattoir. His Serene Highness will then be taken in the dog-catcher's sidecar to the shunting yard, where he will be given a seat in the guard's van. En route, His Serene Highness will share the guard's sandwiches, washed down with a firkin of pear cider. At Clapham Junction, His Serene Highness will be greeted by the representative of the Honourable Charles Knothole – Sid Boggs, the gamekeeper – and will then proceed by tandem to Fred's Pull Up for Carmen in Cheyne Walk. There he will get a warm meat pie and very likely ptomaine poisoning as well. However, if you do decide on Category D one thing is certain, Sir Bertrand.

SIR BERTRAND: And what's that, Codpiece?

CODPIECE: The British Ambassador in Gob will be shot on sight.

SIR BERTRAND: *(Pausing)* Who is the Ambassador out there, Codpiece?

CODPIECE: Sir Hector Bastard. *(He pronounces it 'Bus-stard')* You remember, sir. You were his fag at Eton.

SIR BERTRAND: *(Thoughtfully)* Quite so, Codpiece. *(Decisively)* Category D it is!

I found that Quickies are invaluable in putting together revues, television programmes and even cabaret. I've never met a performer who liked cabaret but, sadly, with the slow disappearance of theatres, the club date has largely taken the place of properly-built auditoriums designed to provide the best presentation for the players. It's amazing how managements seem to put obstacles in the way of the performer: bad sound equipment and dim lighting or, worse still, psychedelic lighting effects and obstructed lines-of-sight for the audience, which all contrive to diminish the performance. I once played to a *large mirror* in order to reach the audience in an L-shaped cabaret room.

It is a triumph to watch real performers (without tricky and deafeningly loud backing) capture and hold their audience right through to a standing ovation. For this kind of show (presented as a show) the 'Quickie' is worth its weight in treacle.

SOME MORE QUICKIES

UP PERISCOPE

The stage is blacked out except for a dull red light contained in a small area. A sonar effect is played in over dramatic music. Two American naval officers, dressed in informal drill jackets and trousers, stand facing each other.

COMMANDER: Up periscope!

(The Lieutenant with him clicks his fingers and the periscope – a large cardboard or plastic tube, equipped with 'snap-down' handles – is dropped into the red-spotted area. The Commander pulls down the two handle-bar type controls and, tipping his hat well back on his head, leans forward and peers intently into the periscope eyepiece, circling one full turn as he does so. At the end of the circle he straightens up and shakes his head)

COMMANDER: I don't like it. Take a look, Lieutenant!
LIEUTENANT: Aye, aye, sir!

(He now replaces the Commander at the periscope – peering into the eyepiece as he, in turn, circles the instrument, stopping at one point and then continuing on until he also completes the move. He stands upright, shaking his head)

COMMANDER: Well, Lieutenant, what do you make of it?

LIEUTENANT: No doubt about it, sir. We're in dry dock.

EIGHTEENTH-CENTURY DUEL

The stage is darkened except for a pool of light where two men in eighteenth-century pirate costume are playing cards on an upturned barrel. They are both extravagantly dressed with feathered tricorne hats and in their broad sashes each pirate carries a flintlock pistol. The atmosphere is tense and suddenly one of them spreads his cards on the barrel head and grabs the pile of coins. The other pirate reacts suspiciously, and lays a restraining hand on the other's sleeve.

SECOND PIRATE: Belay there, Black Bart! I've a mind that you're acheatin' me.

FIRST PIRATE: *(Snarls)* No man calls me a cheat and lives.

(The two pirates kick back the stools on which they have been sitting and circle the barrel, with their hands hovering round the butts of their sash-holstered flintlocks)

SECOND PIRATE: Whenever 'ee be ready, Black Bart, draw!

(The other nods – and then almost simultaneously they both draw their pistols and frenziedly proceed to load them. This requires a quick succession of movements, as they pour in the powder and ram it down, then put the patch of cloth round the lead ball and ram that down the barrel, finally priming the flash pan of the flintlock and clicking the hammer back. Only then can Black Bart fire, just ahead of his duelling opponent. As the flintlock flashes forth in a cloud of smoke and flame (we used electrically-operated pistols and flash powder), the Second Pirate clutches his chest and sways agonizedly, dropping his pistol from a nerveless hand)

SECOND PIRATE: *(Collapsing)* Damn ye, Black Bart! Ye were always *faster* than me!

(He crashes to the ground)

THE ART CRITICS

Here is a gentle radio Quickie (which I have also done on television, by hanging empty frames in a line in front of the camera, which 'crabbed' along the backs of the picture frames, viewing the critics through them as they passed from picture to picture.

The double talk that I have heard and read issuing from the mouths and pens of art critics, is my subject here.

A gallery background of subdued coughing and softly strolling shoes.

ANNOUNCER: Today the Summer Exhibition opened at the Royal
    Academy. Before the general public were allowed to see the exhibits,
    a special viewing was arranged for art critics.

(Footsteps on parquet – two pairs. They stop)

FIRST CRITIC: Ah, yes! *(Reluctantly)*
SECOND CRITIC: And – no!
FIRST CRITIC: Quite so! I like the horse . . .
SECOND CRITIC: And the house.
FIRST CRITIC: In the field.
SECOND CRITIC: With the dog.
FIRST CRITIC: No! *Not* the dog.

(The two pairs of feet move on over the parquet to the next picture)

FIRST CRITIC: *(Stopping)* Ah! Now *there's* a dog!
SECOND CRITIC: And a horse.
FIRST CRITIC: In the field.
SECOND CRITIC: With the house.
FIRST CRITIC: I think not! No! Not the house!

(Again the two pairs of footsteps move on and stop)

FIRST CRITIC: Ah! Now that's what I call a house!
SECOND CRITIC: In the field.
FIRST CRITIC: With the dog.
SECOND CRITIC: And the horse. Excellent!
FIRST CRITIC: But I don't like the gorilla.
SECOND CRITIC: *(Hesitantly)* I don't see a gorilla.
FIRST CRITIC: There! At the bottom. The gorilla.
SECOND CRITIC: That's the signature.
FIRST CRITIC: That's interesting. A picture by a gorilla!
SECOND CRITIC: Yes! Quite excellent! *(Pause)* For a gorilla.

THE LETTER

Here is one of the shortest sketches I ever used. Let's take the radio version.

*A scratching quill pen on a parchment paper, with Florentine music on the lute in
the background.*

WRITER: *(Reading the words as he writes)* My dear Lucretia Borgia, last night's party was delightful. The dinner was superb. I so enjoyed the mushrooms. Aagh! *(Sound of a body falling)*

ENCOUNTER IN MOSCOW

A keening wind and distant sparse traffic.

COMMENTATOR: *(His voice lowered and tense)* Dateline Moscow, and this is Kenneth Mope with another inside story. The Red Square is deserted in the bitter cold, and a light snow shower is falling. Ah, here comes a lone figure. Excuse me, sir, I'm from the British Broadcasting Corporation. Do you speak English?
VOICE: *(Nervously subdued)* Yes.
KENNETH: Do you object to being interviewed?
VOICE: *(Pausing thoughtfully – then answers cautiously)* No.
KENNETH: Can you speak freely?
VOICE: *(Even more subdued, almost whispering)* Yes.
KENNETH: Splendid! Now, what is your name and what is your job?
VOICE: *(Circumspectly)* Jones. I'm the British Ambassador.

THE INVENTOR

This is a send-up of all those Hollywood inspirational films about great inventors and discoverers, whose theme is that 'without-the-inspiration-of-a-woman' the struggling inventor would never have succeeded in bringing some great benefit to mankind.

Paris (for once without the Eiffel Tower). Framed in the window of a dingy attic room, in some poverty-stricken part of the great city, is Notre Dame Cathedral. Dawn is breaking and we find the Inventor, dishevelled and bewhiskered, slumped over his drawing-board, after having been engaged in an all-night session of heavy inventing. Appropriate French atmosphere music is in the background. The garret door opens and in bustles a pretty woman with a basket. She is wearing eighteenth-century clothes. We now see that the Inventor has his hair tied back in a pony tail, secured with grubby black ribbon, and that he is wearing a 'ballet' type shirt with floppy sleeves.

THE GIRL: Chéri, you have been working all night. *(She scolds him gently)*

See, I have brought you petit déjeuner. *(She produces a long French loaf and a pot of steaming coffee from her basket)*

INVENTOR: *(Wearily)* Oui, chérie. I have wrestled with the problems all night and still I have not got the answer. *(Despairingly)* It's no good. I am a failure.

(The girl puts her arms round him as he sits with heaving shoulders at his drawing-board. She lifts her face into a convenient shaft of sunlight which springs into being from behind Notre Dame)

THE GIRL: Courage, my darling! I know you will succeed. You have worked so hard and for so long. Don't let your spirit fail you now, when you are so close to success.

(The haggard face of the Inventor lifts up to show that a glimmer of hope is beginning to dawn upon it)

THE GIRL: *(Passionately)* I have faith in you, my love. Come, my sweet. *(An angel choir starts to swell behind the shaft of sunlight)* Try just *once* more! For me! *(Pause)* For us!

(They embrace and kiss passionately)

INVENTOR: You are right, chérie! *(With growing enthusiasm)* There *must* be a way. Come, I will show you how far I have got with my invention.

(Grabbing the girl's arm, he hurries her over to a shrouded structure in the corner and pulls the cover from it. It is the guillotine)

INVENTOR: Yes, that's it! The *trigger* mechanism! It is set at the wrong angle. *(He adjusts it)* Now!

(The blade thunders down)

INVENTOR: *(Hysterically)* It works! My vegetable slicer works!

(The two of them embrace ecstatically, as a massed choir bursts into the 'Marseillaise')

THE DISCOVERY OF FIRE

COMMENTATOR: Legend hath it that Prometheus brought down fire from heaven. But the truth is far simpler. It was *man* who discovered fire!

(Dramatic music and howling gale sound effects, lightning and thunder. The scene is a cave – dark and starkly bare, except for a rush-strewn floor)

181

COMMENTATOR: *(If this sketch is for radio)* Thousands of years ago, two of our cold and miserable ancestors huddled together for warmth in their cave; their only barrier against death by freezing – fur skins, in which they were wrapped! Their sole protection against the savage beasts outside – primitive stone axes!

(The teeth of the two men chatter with cold)

COMMENTATOR: *(Or 'action', if the sketch is visually presented)* Suddenly their stone axes clashed together as they shivered in the freezing night air.

(Sound effect of striking flints and sparks, then the smouldering and crackling of flames)

COMMENTATOR: *(Or 'action')* The sparks from their axes fell upon the dry rushes on the floor of the cave *(Terrific musical 'sting')* and FIRE WAS BORN!

TWO STONE-AGE MEN: *(Chortling with awe)* Ugh! Ugh! Ugh! Ugh! Ugh!

COMMENTATOR: *(Or 'action')* Disbelieving the evidence of their own eyes, our ancestors tried to touch this new miracle.

ONE STONE-AGE MAN: Ugh! Ooh! *(He draws back his finger and sucks it)* Ooh-ugh! Ooh!

BOTH STONE-AGE MEN: *(Appreciating the warmth)* Ooh! Aah! Ugh-aah! Ooh! etc.

COMMENTATOR: *(Or 'action')* They both tried to find a way of expressing their wonder – to give a name to this marvellous new thing.

FIRST STONE-AGE MAN: *(Tentatively)* Ugh-uh-Gy-er?

SECOND STONE-AGE MAN: *(Shaking his shaggy head)* Ner! er-ugh-er-Dy-er?

FIRST STONE-AGE MAN: Ner! Nigh! *(Thinks hard as he warms himself, front and back, then inspiration strikes)* Ugh-er-Fy-Fy! Fy?

SECOND STONE-AGE MAN: *(Brightens up and encourages his friend as though they were playing 'The game')* Ya! Ya! Ugh! Fy-Fy!

FIRST STONE-AGE MAN: Fy!-Fy! Fy-*yer! yer! Fy!-yer!*

SECOND STONE-AGE MAN: *(Now imbecilic with triumphant joy)* FY-ER! FY-ER!

(They both jump up and down, somersaulting like apes)

BOTH: FYER! FYER! FYER!

(Sound of Stone-Age fire engine arriving and heavy hose putting out the fire. On stage I have used the tag of a Stone-Age fireman complete with brass helmet and stone bucket, dousing the flames)

FATHER'S FOOTSTEPS

The low beams of the backroom workshop emphasize the country craftsman nature of the scene. The battered old workbench, with a row of neatly stacked tools, and the sawdust-strewn floor instantly communicate rustic harmony. A musical background of 'Greensleeves' is playing. Standing at the work bench is an old craftsman, his silver hair and steel-rimmed spectacles perched well down his nose, redolent of simple honest cottage professionalism. His gnarled old hands hold two oddly-shaped pieces of twisted metal, obviously tools of some ancient craft. Beside him is a younger man, also dressed in a sober working-vest and trousers, with a bibbed apron over his chest. Both speak in broad Mummerset.

ELDER CRAFTSMAN: Son, today is a very special day for me, because today I am going to hand over to you in the rightful line of succession – to *you*, Zechariah – the tools of our great craft: what my father afore me and 'is father afore 'im and 'is father afore 'is father . . . *(He is nearly overcome with emotion and his son hurriedly interrupts comfortingly)*

ZECHARIAH: Dad, oi appreciate the solemnity of this moment and oi am proud to be the one to carry the tradition on from a great craftsman – moi Dad!

183

(They embrace, the elder craftsman still clutching the ancient tools of his age-old trade, which bite into the younger man's body)

ZECHARIAH: *(Wincing)* Now, Dad, don't 'ee take on so! *(He carefully guides his father's trembling tool-laden hands away from his vital parts)* Oi'm ready to take on my responsibilities.

ELDER CRAFTSMAN: *(Controlling his emotions with an effort)* Then, Zechariah, *(He hands his son the first weird piece of twisted metal)* here's moi own grindlin' fork – and here *(He hands the other oddly shaped instrument to his successor)* 'ere be moi own favourite nurdlin' 'ammer!

(The younger craftsman takes both tools reverently in hand, his eyes alight with honest craftsman's pride)

ZECHARIAH: *(Almost whispering)* Oh, Dad! Your very own grindlin' fork – and *(His eyes glow with love)* your special nurdlin' 'ammer. *(He inspects them with keen professional appraisal)* Oi tell 'ee, Dad, oi'll always try to live up to the tenets of our ancient craft. I swear it *(He holds the two strange tools at arm's length)* by the grindlin' fork and the nurdlin' 'ammer! *(Thunder and lightning effects outside the window)* By Thor, the first tool maker! *(More thunder)*

ELDER CRAFTSMAN: *(Wisely)* Ah, Zechariah! See that you keep faith with the olde ones!

ZECHARIAH: *(More thunder and lighting)* Ah! *The olde ones!* Ah!

(Father and son embrace, and Zechariah kneels to receive his father's blessing)

ELDER CRAFTSMAN: *(Reverently)* Oh, Lord, guide these, my son Zechariah's young hands in the wise ways of the old craft. In the paths of righteousness and by the tenets and laws of our ancient craft! So mote it be!

ZECHARIAH: So mote it be! *(Pause)* I'll go and change, Dad. *(He disappears behind an ancient screen)*

ELDER CRAFTSMAN: *(Proudly)* The Gods be with 'ee, lad! In all the troils and tribylations of the great craft!

(Zechariah reappears, wearing a spotless white coat and without further words opens the door of the old workroom, calling through it)

ZECHARIAH: Nurse, I'll see Mrs Robinson next. Oh, and I'll need the X-rays of her upper left molars. *(He hands the grindlin' fork and nurdlin' hammer to someone beyond the door)*

ZECHARIAH: Oh, and Nurse! Sterilize these instruments!

184

The BBC can pat itself on its broad back for having pioneered radio and television broadcasting as an aid to learning languages.

For a whole series of radio programmes to Latin America, I played Martin, the Englishman, in *Martin and Maria*. The programme content was in English and Spanish, and Jorge Mora, a South American producer in the BBC Overseas Service, did a fine job on this gentle domestic series. Leda Cacares, an Argentinian, played Maria, and our small team was completed by Peter, another 'Brit' actor. It was all very light-hearted and I had to learn most of the Castilian Spanish like a *papagayo* (a parrot), watched over anxiously by Leda and Jorge.

FRENCH FOR BEGINNERS

I still have the Spanish vocabulary of a Peruvian child, and not long ago accepted our Ambassador's kind invitation to dinner with the Castilian equivalent of: 'Yes, we'd love to have din-dins with you!'

I also once declared enthusiastically that Peru needed: 'Mas invertidos estrangeros,' being under the blissful misapprehension that this meant: 'More foreign investment'.

The Ambassador tactfully pointed out that what I had advocated for a brighter future for Peru was actually: 'More foreign homosexuals'! Oh, I don't know, though!

Encouraged by my efforts at teaching languages by radio, I wrote this sketch.

The living-room and kitchen of a small apartment in Paris. Traditionally, with such a setting we can see the Eiffel Tower through the kitchen window. The strains of a French waltz enhance the gay 'Parisian' atmosphere. A bustling French housewife is standing at the sink washing up. She is wearing a black négligé and black high-heeled shoes. Into the foreground (either visually or on sound perspective) walks our linguistic guide – confident, superior and patronizing.

GUIDE: Voici! Nous sommes dans l'appartement de Monsieur et Madame Dubois! *(He translates)* Here we are in the apartment of Mr and Mrs Wood. *(He continues)* Madame Dubois fait le ménage. *(His speech is very deliberate and precise)* Madame Dubois is doing the housework.

(Madame drops a dish and it breaks loudly)

MADAME: Zut, alors! Espèce de chameau! Crottes de bique!

GUIDE: Oh, dear! Sort of camel – er – goat, poh-pooh!

MADAME: *(Sings)* Frère Jacques, Frère Jacques, dormez vous? Dormez vous? Sonnez les matines! Sonnez les matines! Ding! Dang! Dong! Ding! Dang! Dong!

GUIDE: Brother Jack! Brother Jack! Are you sleeping? Sound the bell, and let's have a ding-dong!

(The door opens and Monsieur Dubois enters. He is wearing the usual misconception of a typical Parisian's outfit – black plastic raincoat over a striped apache sweat-shirt and a beret)

GUIDE: Ah! Voici Monsieur Dubois! Here is Mr Wood!

MADAME: Oh, 'allo, Henri.

GUIDE: Oh, hello, Henry.

HENRI: 'Allo, Clothilde.

GUIDE: Hello, Clothilde.

(The French couple go into a passionate clinch, Henri practically swallowing Clothilde and vice-versa – all with much panting and Gallic oohs! and aahs!)

GUIDE: *(Brightly)* Henry and Clothilde have not been married very long.

MADAME: *(Extricating herself)* Oh, chéri. Tu es de bonne heure. Quelle surprise!

HENRI: Oui, chérie!

GUIDE: Oh, darling. Thou art early, what a surprise. Er, yes darling.

(Henri notices the presence of the linguistic guide whom he doesn't know and certainly doesn't expect)

HENRI: *(Bristling suspiciously)* Eh, qui est là-bas? *(He indicates the guide)*

GUIDE: *(Translating as usual)* Eh, who is that? There.

MADAME: *(Peering short-sightedly, but equally surprised at the very British guide who is holding a microphone)* Qui? Où?

GUIDE: Who? Where?

HENRI: *(In disbelief)* Là, là! Voilà!

GUIDE: *(As though comforting Madame)* There, there! Over there!

HENRI: *(Furiously)* Cet imbecile au coin avec un micro. Pourquoi le micro? Quelle perversion!

GUIDE: *(Still blissfully translating)* That imbecile in the corner with a microphone. Why the microphone? What a perversion!

MADAME: *(Becoming alarmed at Henri's mounting fury)* Non, non, Henri! Je n'ai pas vu cet imbecile. Jamais, jamais, jamais!

GUIDE: No, no, Henri! I have never set eyes on that imbecile. Never, never, never!

HENRI: *(Berserk)* Tu crois que je suis un idiot – un crétin! J'arrive chez moi de bonne heure et je te trouve avec ton amant!

GUIDE: Thou thinkest that I am an idiot! I arrive home early to find you with your lover!

(Henri pulls out a revolver from a drawer)

MADAME: *(Horrified)* Non, non, Henri! Pas ton revolver!

GUIDE: No, no, Henry! Not your revolver!

HENRI: Salaud!

GUIDE: Er – dirty dog!

(Henri fires, and the linguistic expert crashes to the apartment floor)

MADAME: Oh, mon Dieu, Henri!

(Henri walks over to the prostrate guide and turns him over with his foot)

HENRI: *(Hoarsely)* Il est mort! *(Looks up at the camera or speaks directly into the microphone. Deliberately translating)* He – is – dead!

When the show *It's a Square World* unanimously won the Grand Prix de la Presse at the Montreux Television Festival in 1963 I was as surprised as anyone. At the start, the programme had been shown to an empty conference room – until the word got round that here was something different. Then quickly the room filled with enthusiastic competitors, who seemed to forget their rivalry and cheered and applauded the show to the echo.

THE BATTLE OF THE BANDS

It was a wonderful moment. Various people have since told me that we would also have walked off with the Golden Rose of Montreux but, as I have mentioned before, the gag that I had put in (of Khrushchev pounding his desk at the United Nations to the tune of 'Black Eyes') was too much for the Russian contingent. No matter, the 'Press' prize is the one given from the heart – without political undertones – so I was more than content.

The finale of the Montreux edition of *It's a Square World* was the musical memoirs of the British Army's Director of Music. This is the piece that apparently decided the International Press.

A typical, stark 1960s interview set-up suitable for 'in-depth', face-to-face trials by television. Behind the two functional chairs is a projection screen and the grim-faced interviewer stands in front of a table loaded with books, which are standing up with their covers facing the audience. Their titles, in several languages, all mean 'Battle Symphony'.

INTERVIEWER: *(Holding one of the books)*: Battle Symphony is more than just a book. It is the latest in a long line of war memoirs – but this one is different. Here in the studio tonight, we have the author – Brigadier-General Sir Maxwell Beetby, DSO, RACM, Musicians' Union.

GENERAL: And bar!

INTERVIEWER: He is the British Army's Director of Music.

GENERAL: Good evening. *(He turns and salutes)*

INTERVIEWER: *Battle Symphony* is a major work, General. It shows us a new side of war – grim and enthralling but somehow – er – er – *(He searches for the word)*

GENERAL: Harmonious?

INTERVIEWER: *(Uncertainly)* Well, I suppose so!

GENERAL: *(Interrupting)* War is hell! A series of discords with a continually altering tempo. Bruto! Large tacit periods and then the Allegro con brillo and before you can say Allegro ma non troppo it's all crescendo to the finale – forte, fortissimo – right to the last tympany roll and the ultimate cymbal crash! I've conducted a few musical battles in my time and I can tell you, sir, war *is* hell – usually in C sharp minor.

INTERVIEWER: Quite so! *(He is relieved at getting the ball back)* You were of course on the Army's musical reserve in 1939 when the war started. Can . . .?

GENERAL: *(Interrupting again)* Quite right! As the opening chords of battle rolled across Europe, I had already been called back to the colours and I was immediately put in charge of the Army's School of Music at Kneller Hall. The situation was grim, I can tell you. *(The interviewer can't get a word in edgeways)* There was my old team playing instruments that had long ago been discarded by our enemies. *(Proudly)* My lads were risking their umbishas on brass instruments that were obsolete by 1918.

(Behind him we see film of the German Army bands marching down the Unter den Linden)

GENERAL: *(Dramatically)* While the enemy on the other hand rehearsed to a man, trained to concert pitch, equipped with the very latest instruments that Hun ingenuity could devise. When I saw those bands marching down the Unter den Linden in Berlin, I knew that we were in for a long and bitter struggle for musical supremacy.

INTERVIEWER: *(Diving in)* What about your own men, General?

GENERAL: As usual, British politicians had unscrupulously cut the British Army's musical budget to the bone. Even our Royal Trumpeters had to practise with their mouthpieces only – their trumpets were too valuable to risk on rehearsal. And as for the new recruits – well, the spirit was as ever willing, but *(Brokenly)* the instruments were whatever we could get.

(On the back projection screen we see the recruits, still in civilian clothes, marching, blowing Kazoos and playing on paper and combs)

GENERAL: Magnificent spirit, what?

(We see him taking the salute outside Kneller Hall, standing on the marble steps of the Army's School of Music, flanked on either side by large tubas on stone plinths, marked 'Captured at Sebastopol')

GENERAL: But by 1940 the tempo had changed. Long and exhausting rehearsals had brought my men up to the pitch where they could face the enemy with a chance. Lease-Lend from our friends in the United States had brought us new instruments, some of which even worked. Then the Intermezzo was over and we were thrown straight into the Battle Symphony. North Africa!

(The film now takes over as the cameras zoom in on troop-transports loading and a convoy of ships anchored off Gibraltar, dissolving into a map of North Africa and pulling out to show the word Tobruk. *As the scene changes to a desert wadi with a large sand-bagged redoubt, we see a military band tuning up. It is the only sound above the light keening of the desert wind. The troops are now dressed in tin hats, khaki-drill jackets and Empire shorts, long socks and 'desert creeper' boots)*

GENERAL: *(Raising a camouflaged baton)* Right lads! 'Colonel Bogey' in the key of C.

(The troops play a passable version of the 'Immortal Colonel' and are cut off in mid-note by the General)

GENERAL: *(Peevishly)* Blasted sand. Gets everywhere. Take five to oil your instruments. We must be prepared, lads. The enemy may launch a major musical offensive at any moment. Keep your eyes peeled and your ears open for the opening bars of 'The Ride of the Valkyries'.

(The General cautiously peers over the parapet of the sand-bagged desert fort and scans the horizon through his binoculars. In his other hand is a cup of tea. The camera whizz-pans up to the skyline where a lone German trombonist is lying among the sand dunes, a telescopic sight fitted to his instrument. A metal clip holds the small music manuscript card to the trombone. He is an advanced musical sniper. Through the telescopic sight the German centres on the General and we see from the Nazi's point of view the cross hairs of his sights)

GENERAL: *(Muttering to himself)* I wonder what the Hun is up to?

(The German sniper trombonist blows a single loud blast on his instrument and the General's teacup shatters)

GENERAL: *(Ducking)* Damn it, lads! Keep as tacit as you can – this looks like a sneak attack. *(The sound of Stuka dive bombers is now heard)* Great Scott! Take cover, lads! Keep your instruments out of sight!

(We cut to a flight of swastikaed German Junker 86 dive bombers – the famous Stukas)

GENERAL: It's the Stukas! Hang on, lads!

(The dive bombers peel off and wing over in a screaming dive-bomb attack in a vertical line – releasing their bombs at the end of the pullout. The British musicians hug the dirt, as the redoubt rocks with giant musical chords. When the smoke and dust clears and the sound of 'The Ride of the Valkyries' has faded away, the General stands up and surveys the scene while much coughing is heard.

GENERAL: Anyone hurt, Sergeant-Major?
WELSH SERGEANT-MAJOR: Indeed to goodness, nobody, sir. All present and correct, sir, at all, at all.

GENERAL: I thought you Welsh fusiliers used the words 'look you' at the end of each passage?

WELSH SERGEANT-MAJOR: My mother was Irish, sir!

GENERAL: Well, lads! It looks like the concert is warming up. *(He suddenly sees something outside the parapet and hurries over to the sand-bags for a closer look)* Good heavens! It's an unexploded German double bass!

(We now see that stuck halfway into the sand is a large double bass with bomb-type tail fins marked with swastikas)

GENERAL: I want a volunteer to help me defuse it.

WELSH SERGEANT-MAJOR: I'll volunteer, sir! I did a course on German violas and stringed booby traps!

GENERAL: Good show, Sergeant-Major! Follow me!

(He slithers over the parapet and they both crawl towards the smoking double-bass bomb)

GENERAL: *(As the Sergeant-Major gets a stethoscope on to the bass fiddle)* Well? Is it live?

(A clear ticking can be heard. The Sergeant-Major listens to it, beating time with his hand)

SERGEANT-MAJOR: It's live, sir! Alla breve time, sir!

(The General vanishes behind the parapet, as we 'frame-cut' the film to make him disappear. Then from the parapet he calls softly)

GENERAL: *(Seriously)* Can you handle it alone, Sergeant-Major?
SERGEANT-MAJOR: I'll try, sir.

(He carefully takes out a pair of pliers and cuts the strings one by one. They part with a sharp musical twang – in the appropriate key, of course. He then carefully opens the side of the double-bass bomb and takes out a metronome attached to the belly of the bass by wires. Cautiously the Sergeant-Major examines the tempo scale)

SERGEANT-MAJOR: It's set at common time, sir!
GENERAL: Careful, Sergeant-Major! It may be booby trapped.
SERGEANT-MAJOR: Don't worry, sir. *(He snips the wires and the metronome stops ticking. He stands up and salutes)* It's defused, sir! *(He salutes smartly, loudly stamping his feet as he does so, and the double bass blows up in the key of A flat as a major chord/explosion drowns out everything)*
GENERAL: Dear God! *(As the smoke clears, we see that only a pair of smoking boots remain at attention. The sound of a celestial cadenza on a harp is heard ascending towards the Great Musicians' Concert Hall in the sky. The General salutes the gallant Sergeant-Major)*
GENERAL: Come on, lads! They must have heard that last chord. They'll be attacking at any moment. Moderato, chaps! Moderato!

(As they listen tensely for the opening bars of the German Philharmonic Panzer Brigade, we hear the sound of approaching tanks – and cut to a stock shot of German Panzers on the move in North Africa)

GENERAL: Right, men! All in tune?
MEN: Yes, sir! Right, sir! Give us an A, Fred!
GENERAL: Wait till you see the whites of their trombone mutes!

(An approaching armoured car with the turret lid open contains General Von Zwei Drei, the great German Panzer conductor)

GERMAN GENERAL: Halt! *(He scans the distant British desert redoubt through his binoculars)* Ach so! Der britische Tommy-Orchester-General. Der General Beetby, yes! *(He gives an order)* Feuer! Konzertklang C!

(Two German tuba players prepare to fire explosive trombone and trumpet mutes, using their tubas as mortars. One German musician slides the mutes down the large tuba bell and a big fat German musician blows them out! The mutes explode near the redoubt with a loud tuba note)

BRITISH GENERAL: *(Ducking below the sand-bags)* Corporal! Fire smoke in E flat!

(A British musician fires his trombone like a bazooka. As his buddy loads it up the bell end with a mute, the musician blows it out with distended cheeks and an extended slide. The mute explodes against the German Concert Grand Tank and heavy white smoke pours out of the mute. The Germans fire back. Smoke starts to build up in the desert wadi)

GENERAL: Right, men! It's 'The British Grenadiers' and then straight into 'Colonel Bogey'. With a one-two – one-two-three-four.

(As he waves his baton the small British band breaks into the strains of the famous marches. Overhead a flight of troop-carrying Dakotas (DC 3s) appears, and the General watches them through his binoculars)

GENERAL: *(Much relieved as he continues to conduct)* It's an air drop, lads.

(Cheers from the British musicians and a pause in the music as we cut to the interior of a Dakota, where a small detachment of airborne musicians in full parachutists' gear are hooked on ready for the drop. They are led by a Scottish Sergeant Pipe Major, dressed in a kilt and holding his bagpipes like a sub-machinegun)

SERGEANT: Right, my bonny boys. Green light! Trombone out!

(The trombonist blows a note or two and continues to play as he jumps)

SERGEANT: Trumpet out!

(The trumpet player does the same)

SERGEANT: Drummer out!

(The drummer jumps, beating his drum)

SERGEANT: Fife out!

(The fife player vanishes with a disappearing trill)

SERGEANT: Me out!

(The Pipe Major starts up his bagpipes and jumps – and we hear the wail of his pipes echoing down the blue. The Germans are watching all this activity and getting ready to attack – their trombones and trumpets sticking out of their armoured car. The German General is at the head of a small patrol detachment of heavy brass playing musicians. Back at the British redoubt the Scottish Pipe Major salutes the British General)

SERGEANT: Pipe Major MacDangle reporting, sir! *(His bagpipes are now carried at the 'slope')*

GENERAL: *(Saluting back)* Very good, Pipe Major! 'Colonel Bogey' in the key of C! Lead the advance!

SERGEANT: Very good, sir!

(He puts the pipes to his lips and blows away until the drones screech into the Scottish version of the march. Away he goes into the boiling battle smoke. As he vanishes, there is the sound of a shot and the bagpipes stop with a dying whine. After a moment, the Pipe Major reappears staggering back through the billowing clouds)

PIPE MAJOR: Stretcher bearers!

(Two medics rush towards him with a stretcher. Tenderly the Pipe Major lays his stricken bagpipes on the stretcher and covers them with a blanket. Then he straightens up and salutes the wounded pipes as the medics hurry away)

GENERAL: *(Handing the Pipe Major a small cornet)* Never mind, Pipe Major! Lead the attack with this!

SERGEANT: *(Very moved)* Thank you very much, sir.

(He raises the cornet to his lips and faces the enemy with a smart about-turn. Then, as the General conducts, the Pipe Major advances, blowing on his cornet – but making exactly the same sound as though he were playing the bagpipes)

GENERAL: My God, I'll recommend that man for the Royal Academy of
   Music's Gold Medal! *(To his band)* Forward! The Guards!

*(The entire band advances over the sand-bagged parapet, playing 'Colonel Bogey'
energetically. There now follows a musical mêlée which is dramatically highlighted
by the smoke and fog of the battle area. A veritable Battle of the Bands! As the
British, led by their conducting General, march into the swirling clouds, we mix
through to the German band playing 'The Ride of the Valkyries' and conducted by
their leather-coated, jack-booted orchestra master General)*

BRITISH GENERAL: *(Voice over)* As my gallant lads headed the great attack
   at El Alamein the battle became confused. We could hardly see each
   other in the thick smoke.

*(We see the British band vanishing into the smoke – then the German General leads
his band out of the darkness. He looks confused and about-turns his 'Valkyries'-
playing band back into the smoke. 'Colonel Bogey' becomes the dominant music*

again and this time the British General appears, but at the head of the German *band! He hastily about-turns and leads them back into the battle clouds.*

'The Valkyries' now dominate the scene, and out of the fog comes the German General conducting the British *band, who are now playing the German music. They retire into the smoke. Finally both the British and German Generals appear wearing each other's helmets and totally confused, as they conduct both their bands playing 'Colonel Bogey' and 'The Valkyries' at one and the same time . . . We fade the battle scene and come up on the Victory Parade down Pall Mall in London with stock shots of the massed marching Allied troops and cheering crowds)*

BRITISH GENERAL: *(Voice over)* But soon it was all over. VE Day was upon us and the lads came marching home to a triumphant welcome.

(Cut to two small children waving flags)

INTERVIEWER: And now you are in retirement, General Beetby?

GENERAL: Indeed! But you can't keep an old musical war-horse down. I'm kept busy conducting Gilbert and Sullivan for the British Retired Servicemen's Bands, Boy Scout Rallies and that sort of thing. Oh, and my old war comrade, the German General Von Zwei Drei, comes to stay with me and we swop manuscripts. We're jointly conducting *The Pirates of Penzance* for the retired Hitler Youth Orchestra. We're the guests of the National Front.

INTERVIEWER: And your men, sir? Your old battle comrades – what's happened to them?

GENERAL: Ah, yes! The *men*! They're still together, enjoying the rewards that a grateful British Government always gives to her war heroes.

(As he speaks, we cut to a street scene, where the 'men' in faded civilian clothes, wearing mufflers and grubby cloth caps and clinking campaign medals, are wearily shuffling along the gutter, playing unpolished and battered instruments. The Pipe Major rattles a collecting box and one or two passers-by put in a few pence. This pathetic scene suddenly changes as a very pretty girl puts her pennies in the box. The band smartens up and, still playing, chases the lovely lass off the screen, round the Houses of Parliament and eventually right through the projection screen itself, pursuing the glamorous blonde among the studio audience, as we roll credit titles and segue into the title music)

199

It struck me that with all the massive training programmes the KGB carries out, there remains one area of indoctrination at Soviet spy schools that is sadly lacking.

No matter how well-versed a Soviet secret agent may be in the techniques of clandestine operations, the lack of a sense of humour of the kind enjoyed in his Western democratic target areas might well cause him to be singled out and his cover blown!

RUSSIAN PRACTICAL JOKES

Intelligence agents of the Second World War told me how imperative it was to be able to fade into the local background of their target areas, and that a knowledge of the local sense of humour was of supreme importance to their success. This sketch is one result of that information. It is not as far-fetched as it seems.

The classroom of a Soviet spy school, somewhere in the Urals. The student agents are seated at desks facing a blackboard-backed rostrum on which there is a table and a chair. As the door opens two KGB uniformed security men accompany a KGB Colonel to his place behind the table. The students rise smartly from their desks and stand at attention. The KGB Colonel removes his cap and places four small boxes down in front of him on the table.

COLONEL: Be seated, comrades. This morning we are going to learn about humour of a highly specialized kind, as practised in the Western democracies, especially in our designated target areas, the British Isles and the United States of America. As usual all instruction will be in the English language and notes will be taken, memorized and then destroyed. You will repeat after me the main points of my lecture. First of all, the title of our subject: British and American Practical Jokes.

STUDENTS: *(In chorus, aloud, while making notes)* British and American Practical Jokes.

COLONEL: First practical joke: black face soap.

STUDENTS: *(Writing hard and repeating the words aloud)* Black face soap.

COLONEL: *(Taking bar of soap out of a small box and reading instructions)* Black face soap . . . *(Pause)* . . . a sure-fire way to get a big laugh.

STUDENTS: *(Busily writing)* Big laugh.

COLONEL: Leave soap in washroom! The victim will use it to wash himself and imagine his surprise when he sees that his face has turned black in the mirror! A real belly laugh for one dollar forty cents.

STUDENTS: *(Muttering)* One dollar forty cents.

COLONEL: *(Opening second small box and taking out a 'blood-stained' nail, which he examines carefully. Reading instructions)* Nail-through-the-finger. Give the gang a real shiver! Place the nail through the finger . . .

STUDENTS: Nail through the finger . . .

COLONEL: . . . on one of your fingers and it will look like you just drove it through your hand. A real rib-tickler! Seventy five cents, plus tax.

STUDENTS: Plus tax.

(The Colonel shrugs at the incomprehensibility of Allied humour and opens the next box. We can't see what is inside, but the Colonel looks at it in disgusted amazement)

COLONEL: *(Reading box lid)* Naughty Doggie! *(He pronounces it 'Nawtiey Dogyiey')* Pooh-Pooh!

(We can see the label, which is unmistakable)

STUDENTS: Naughty Doggy. *(Same pronunciation)* Pooh-Pooh!

COLONEL: *(Unbelieving)* Naughty Doggie Pooh-Pooh is so life-like that, when placed on your host's or hostess's favourite carpet, it will really cause a ruckus! People have even been known to kick their dogs up the ass. A great way to break the ice at any social gathering! Note: only for use in winter. Only one dollar but worth more – much more!

STUDENTS: *(Writing furiously)* Much more.

(The Colonel is still totally mystified but, for the glory of the Soviet Union, he continues – this time picking up a flat rubber bag, equipped with a nozzle, to which is fitted a raspberry blower)

COLONEL: *(Reading instructions on the rubber bag)* Whoopee Cushion.

STUDENTS: Whoopee Cushion.

COLONEL: Inflate Whoopee Cushion! *(Does so)*

STUDENTS: Inflate Whoopee Cushion!

COLONEL: *(Cushion now inflated)* Place Whoopee Cushion beneath the cushion of chair. *(Does so)*

STUDENTS: Beneath cushion of chair.

COLONEL: *(Reading)* When the unsuspecting victim sits down on the hidden Whoopee Cushion, boy, will he get a surprise! A great laugh!

Guaranteed to make you the hit of the evening and just great for the Party!

STUDENTS: *(All stand up)* Long live the Party!

(They all give the left-handed clenched-fist salute)

COLONEL: *(Echoing their words)* Long live the Party!

(Sits down on his inflated Whoopee Cushion which blows a fulsome raspberry with great clarity. The two uniformed KGB guards react immediately and rapidly close in on the demoralized Colonel, grasping him firmly by either arm and virtually carrying him off)

COLONEL: *(Protesting loudly)* Niet! Niet! You don't understand. It is American decadent democratic practical joke.

STUDENTS: Practical joke! Poor bastard!

Over the past thirty-six years of writing comedy, I have found that real-life can't be beaten when it comes to belly laughs.

While performing many of the pieces in this book in front of an audience, or filming and tele-recording others in the streets and fields of Britain, many funny things have happened.

I have written before about my bombarding the Houses of Parliament with cannon balls (sadly only plastic) fired from a

YOU CAN'T TOP LIFE

Chinese junk, while making an episode of *It's a Square World* for the BBC, but it bears repeating. The idea came to me while talking to a friendly Chinese doctor when we were filming in Limehouse (the old traditional Chinatown of London). He was furious, and anything but inscrutable, about the high-handed actions of the then London County Council in tearing down his beloved Chinatown and replacing it with featureless blocks of high-rise apartments.

'I'd like to sink the whole bloody lot of them,' he said angrily.

'How would you do that?' I asked, fascinated by the thought.

'Sink 'em with cannon balls fired from a Chinese war junk, of course.'

A week later I was cruising up the Thames and came across a small Chinese junk, beautifully kept by its owner, an out-of-work actor. The two images coincided in my mind and 'Sinking the Houses of Parliament' went into the next script. For two hours we sailed that suitably decorated and armed Chinese junk up and down outside the House of Commons on the stretch of river above Westminster Bridge, firing polystyrene cannon balls which bounced off the stones of that venerable building. Although we were costumed in full Chinese war-lord outfits and Clive Dunn was dressed up as Dr Fu-Manchu, no one seemed to notice us. One of the patients at St Thomas's Hospital, across the river, even tried hard *not* to see us. He came out on to a balcony in his pyjamas and dressing gown, took one look at the junk, and hastily went back inside.

Eventually a police launch – whose crew must have been informed officially that the BBC were filming in their waters – edged itself alongside the junk and a police sergeant with a loud-hailer asked us: 'Do any of you gentlemen speak English?'

On another occasion I decided to remake *Moby Dick, the Great White Whale*, but this time to have the mighty creature come up the Thames to the quiet waters above

Richmond lock. This idea came when I saw an article in the paper about a small whale which had swum up river and had become stranded underneath Kew Bridge, near Isleworth. All rescue attempts failed and, sadly, the little whale died.

The idea bubbled away in my subconscious and eventually I persuaded my producer, John Street, to do the piece. John, a very experienced director/producer and one of the brains behind the *Benny Hill Shows*, knew that most of my hare-brained schemes worked.

We built a sixty-foot floating white whale and then approached the Thames Conservancy Board for permission to film it on the upper reaches of that lovely river.

The conversation went like this:

OFFICIAL: This 'vessel' that you wish to navigate in our waters – how long is it?
SELF: Sixty feet.
OFFICIAL: *(Writing it all down)* Beam?
SELF: Ten feet.
OFFICIAL: *(Unsuspectingly)* Draught?
SELF: Approximately two foot six inches.
OFFICIAL: Method of propulsion?
SELF: Outboard motor.
OFFICIAL: Is the vessel fitted with a chemical toilet?
SELF: No.
OFFICIAL: *(Sternly)* It will have to be. No sea toilets are allowed above Richmond half-tide lock.
SELF: It shall be done.
OFFICIAL: Now! Is this vessel a launch? A cruiser? Or a narrow boat?
SELF: It's a whale.
OFFICIAL: A *what*?
SELF: A great white whale. Moby Dick.
OFFICIAL: Good morning, Mr Bentine! Close the door on the way out!

So many marvellous things happened during those productive years of *It's a Square World*, *All Square* and *After Hours*.

The 'Pirate Bus' idea came to me as I read a local newspaper from the Portsmouth area. PIRATE BUSES APPEARING ON THE SOUTH COAST, it said in bold type.

The image of open-topped double-decker buses flying the skull and crossbones flag flashed on to the inner screen of my mind. I could see it all quite clearly. Armed with broadsides of cannon they could fight with Royal Navy buses of the Line!

'Long John Silver' versus 'Conductor Horatio Hornblower' – what a sight that would be! So we got two open-topped buses and fixed them up, with great ship's wheels and six cannon apiece – crewed by neatly uniformed Jack Tars of the Nelsonian epoch and swarthy pirates of the Spanish Main. We ran them up and down the front of Seaford, a sleepy retirement resort on the South Coast, and once again nobody took any notice.

As one smoke-scarred and battle damaged 'pirate' bus pulled in for a moment's pause at a request stop, two little old ladies got on it. The conductor, Long John Silver, complete with a wooden leg and a stuffed parrot, tried to dissuade them. 'I'm sorry, madam. This bus is not for carrying passengers. We're filming for the BBC.'

'I see,' said one old dear. 'Well, young man! When is the next one due?'

During those years, I led a canoe expedition up the River Thames to discover its source, which turned out to be a large dripping tap (which we turned off, thereby stranding all the great ships on the mud of the Lower Thames basin), and I headed a 'Russian' climbing expedition to ascend the highest point in Woolwich (in return, presumably, for a Woolwich climbing team conquering the highest mountain peak in Russia). In this case, Woolwich rubbish dump proved to be the tallest and smelliest pinnacle, near the gas works.

I also blew up a 'Food Dump' which had gone *critical* – the chain reaction starting during an attempt to defuse a gigantic Army Christmas pudding, left over from the Boer War.

We even filmed a safari to discover the 'Lost World' of giant bulldozers on a remote plateau, near Barnet in North London. Faced with these great charging beasts, we immobilized one of them by removing the drain plug of its huge gear box – then brought it chained into the studio at Elstree, where it broke loose in panic at the news photographers' flashing lights (the climax of the film *King Kong*).

As it charged the audience, who actually *did* panic, I realized that all through these weird and wonderful escapades the great British public had never once showed anything more than a passing interest in what we were doing. They just didn't want to get involved.

I sank the BBC with a submarine, set it alight during a Red Indian raid, attacked it with a man-eating orchid that had escaped from *Gardening Club*, tunnelled out of the BBC Television Centre in a 'great escape' pursued by BBC Gestapo guards in small Messerschmitt cars – and finally sent the centre itself into orbit, with a commentary by my old friend Patrick Moore. Miracle of miracles – the BBC let me do it!

All those pieces of lunacy were highlighted for me by the reaction of the public to what we were doing. For instance, some time after I'd finished working with BBC Television, a Jaguar drove into the BBC carpark at the Television Centre and men with stocking masks and holding pick-axe handles got out of it and 'did' the cashier's office, escaping with the payroll.

Legend has it that the BBC security guard on duty called out: 'Hello, Mr Bentine. Nice to see you back!'

And as they roared away, he added: 'When is it on?'

That story has to have an element of truth because the robbery followed on the mayhem that I had regularly perpetrated during the five years of making *It's a Square World* at the BBC.